Fintech Revolution and Financial Inclusion in Emerging Markets: Shaping Sustainable Digital Finance

Edited by

Mohammed Majeed
Department of Marketing, Tamale Technical University, Tamale, Ghana

Sofia Devi Shamurailatpam
Department of Banking and Insurance, Faculty of Commerce, The Maharaja Sayajirao University of Baroda, Vadodara, Gujarat, India

Parag Sunil Shukla
Department of Commerce and Business Management, Faculty of Commerce, The Maharaja Sayajirao University of Baroda, Vadodara, Gujarat, India

Ibrahim Osman
Department of Marketing,
Tamale Technical University, Tamale, Ghana

&

Hamidu Gafaru Dokurugu
Department of Entrepreneurship and Enterprise Development, Tamale Technical University, Tamale, Ghana

Fintech Revolution and Financial Inclusion in Emerging Markets: Shaping Sustainable Digital Finance

Editors: Mohammed Majeed, Sofia Devi Shamurailatpam, Parag Sunil Shukla

Ibrahim Osman and Hamidu Gafaru Dokurugu

ISBN (Online): 979-8-89881-315-4

ISBN (Print): 979-8-89881-316-1

ISBN (Paperback): 979-8-89881-317-8

Published by Bentham Science Publishers Pte. Ltd. Singapore,

in collaboration with Eureka Conferences, USA.

First published in 2025.

Bentham Science Publishers Pte. Ltd.
No. 9 Raffles Place
Office No. 26-01
Singapore 048619
Singapore
Email: subscriptions@benthamscience.net

BENTHAM SCIENCE

CONTENTS

FOREWORD

In an era where financial exclusion remains a noteworthy universal task, the arrival of Financial Technology (FinTech) has started a transformative crusade. FinTech not only aims to reform access to financial services but also seeks to fundamentally alter the architecture of financial systems, especially in developing economies. The book, Fintech Revolution and Financial Inclusion, offers a comprehensive examination of how FinTech is narrowing the divide between the unbanked population and conventional financial institutions. While financial inclusion has long been recognized as a crucial factor in fostering economic development and societal welfare, millions worldwide, particularly in less developed regions, still lack access to basic financial services. Conventional banking systems often struggle to reach these underserved communities due to infrastructure constraints, elevated operational costs, and insufficient financial education. However, the proliferation of digital technologies is now creating unparalleled opportunities to address this issue. The uniqueness of this book lies in its holistic approach to investigating the impact of FinTech on promoting financial inclusion in emerging markets. The book's chapters explore how various technologies, ranging from artificial intelligence and machine learning to blockchain and mobile-based solutions, can create new avenues for individuals previously excluded from the financial landscape. This book explores not just the potential of FinTech but also the hurdles encountered during its deployment. The chapter authors meticulously demonstrate that the path from innovation to real-world impact is riddled with challenges, including complex regulations, gaps in digital literacy, and constraints in financial infrastructure. Nevertheless, by tackling these issues directly and emphasizing inclusive, sustainable approaches, we can ensure that digital finance's advantages reach those most in need. By consolidating diverse viewpoints on the convergence of technology, finance, and social progress, this book provides a timely and crucial analysis of FinTech's capacity to effect enduring change in developing markets. The knowledge shared here will prove essential for policymakers, entrepreneurs, academics, and anyone committed to molding the future of sustainable digital finance. The significance of this dialogue cannot be overemphasized. In an ever-evolving world, financial inclusion through innovative FinTech solutions may be the catalyst for economic empowerment, social equity, and environmental sustainability. As we chart the course for finance's future, we must strive to leave no one behind.

Dr. Ahmed Tijani
Corporate Affairs &
Information Technology (IT)
Minerals Commission
Ghana

PREFACE

Of late, the financial sector has experienced a momentous change, pushed by the rapid development of Financial Technology (FinTech) and a wide-reaching effort to enhance financial accessibility. The potential of digital finance is particularly impactful in developing economies, where many still struggle to access conventional banking services. FinTech has created novel possibilities, delivering innovative solutions to underserved communities, enhancing access to credit, savings, and insurance products, and revolutionizing economies that have historically been excluded from mainstream financial systems. This book aims to examine the dynamic convergence of technology, finance, and social inclusion, with a focus on emerging markets. It compiles insights from industry experts, practitioners, and thought leaders, shedding light on FinTech's transformative role in fostering sustainable development, economic empowerment, and financial accessibility. As we explore the future of digital finance, we seek to comprehend how FinTech innovations, such as Artificial Intelligence (AI), blockchain, and mobile banking, can tackle the urgent issues of financial exclusion. Each chapter offers an in-depth analysis of current and future trends shaping the financial inclusion agenda, ranging from empowering ever-married women in India to incorporating Environmental, Social, and Governance (ESG) factors into fintech investments. The path from innovation to real-world impact is fraught with obstacles. Numerous challenges—whether they be technical, legal, or cultural—must be surmounted to ensure digital financial services reach every corner of the world. This volume provides a critical analysis of these hurdles and potential solutions that could lead to a more inclusive and sustainable financial system. We anticipate that this book will motivate scholars, government officials, innovators, and financial sector experts to further investigate FinTech's potential as a positive force in developing economies. The FinTech revolution is only in its early stages, and its ability to transform the financial landscape knows no bounds.

Mohammed Majeed
Department of Marketing,
Tamale Technical University,
Tamale, Ghana

Sofia Devi Shamurailatpam
Department of Banking and Insurance,
Faculty of Commerce, The Maharaja Sayajirao University of Baroda,
Vadodara, Gujarat, India

Parag Sunil Shukla
Department of Commerce and Business Management,
Faculty of Commerce, The Maharaja Sayajirao University of Baroda, Vadodara, Gujarat, India

Ibrahim Osman
Department of Marketing,
Tamale Technical University, Tamale, Ghana

&

Hamidu Gafaru Dokurugu
Department of Entrepreneurship and Enterprise Development, Tamale Technical University, Tamale, Ghana

List of Contributors

Abhishek Kumar Pandey	Department of Management, IILM Academy of Higher Learning, Lucknow, Uttar Pradesh, India
Aditya Keshari	Institute of Management, Nirma University, Ahmedabad, Gujarat, India
Abibu Amidu	Department of Accountancy, Tamale Technical University, Tamale, Ghana
Javid Ahmad Khan	Department of Economics, Islamic University of Science and Technology (IUST), Awantipora, Jammu and Kashmir, India
Kumari Neelam	Department of Commerce, Mahatma Gandhi Kashi Vidyapith University, Varanasi, Uttar Pradesh, India
Mohammad Majeed	Department of Marketing, Tamale Technical University, Tamale, Ghana
Milan Yadav	School of Commerce, Galgotias University, Greater Noida, Uttar Pradesh, India
Manish Kumar Singh	Department of Management, School of Management Sciences, Lucknow, Uttar Pradesh, India
Manisha Pawar	Department of Accounting and Financial Management, Faculty of Commerce, The Maharaja Sayajirao University of Baroda, Vadodara, Gujarat, India
Mudasir Ahmad Sheergujree	Department of Economics, Islamic University of Science and Technology (IUST), Awantipora, Jammu and Kashmir, India
Mohammed Majeed	Department of Marketing, Tamale Technical University, Tamale, Ghana
Nishant Kumar	Deptartment of Management, Faculty of Management Studies, University of Lucknow, Lucknow, Uttar Pradesh, India
Nidhi Upendra Argade	Department of Accounting and Financial Management, Faculty of Commerce, The Maharaja Sayajirao University of Baroda, Vadodara, Gujarat, India
Naorem Pushparani Chanu	School of Liberal Studies and Education, Navrachana University, Vadodara, Gujarat, India
Pankaj Kumar	Faculty of Commerce and Management, United University, Prayagraj, Uttar Pradesh, India
Pramod Kumar Upadhyay	Department of Commerce, Maharaja Bijli Pasi Government P.G. College, University of Lucknow, Lucknow, Uttar Pradesh, India
Rabichandra Singh Elangbam	School of Business and Law, Navrachana University, Vadodara, Gujarat, India
Sofia Devi Shamurailatpam	Department of Banking and Insurance, Faculty of Commerce, The Maharaja Sayajirao University of Baroda, Vadodara, Gujarat, India
Sayed Gulzar Ganai	Department of Economics, Symbiosis International University, Pune, Maharashtra, India
Sofia Devi Shamurailatpam	Department of Banking and Insurance, Faculty of Commerce, The Maharaja Sayajirao University of Baroda, Vadodara, Gujarat, India

Upnishad Mishra	School of Business, Galgotias University, Greater Noida, Uttar Pradesh, India
Umesh Gupta	School of Business and Management Studies, MATS University, Raipur, Chhattisgarh, India
Virendra Singh	Department of Sociology, Faculty of Arts, The Maharaja Sayajirao University of Baroda, Vadodara, Gujarat, India
Vijaya Kittu Manda	Perspectives on Business Management & Economics, Visakhapatnam, Andhra Pradesh, India

CHAPTER 1

Financial Inclusion in Emerging Market Economies: A Macroeconomic Perspective

Sofia Devi Shamurailatpam[1,*] and **Mohammad Majeed**[2]

[1] *Department of Banking and Insurance, Faculty of Commerce, The Maharaja Sayajirao University of Baroda, Vadodara, Gujarat, India*

[2] *Department of Marketing, Tamale Technical University, Tamale, Ghana*

Abstract: This chapter reviews recent trends in financial inclusion and its progress from a macroeconomic perspective, focusing on Emerging Market Economies (EMEs). The importance of EMEs in the global economy is evident in their dynamic and adaptive economic characteristics, especially given the structural challenges they face in integrating with the world economy. Understanding the extent of financial inclusion is crucial, as finance drives economic growth and ensures resource sustainability, in line with the socio-economic policy goals set by regulatory bodies and policymakers in these economies. We have analyzed financial inclusion in 20 selected EMEs based on the World Bank database and various macroeconomic development indicators, shedding light on the fundamental nature of their financial systems. While significant progress has been made in terms of access to finance, as evidenced by the growing number of people with formal bank accounts, there has also been progress in the use of financial services, such as savings, borrowing, and payments. However, concerns remain regarding the quality of services and the affordability of financial products.

Keywords: Accessibility to finance, Emerging market economies, Financial inclusion, Finance-led-growth.

INTRODUCTION

Dominated by dynamic and adaptive economies, Emerging Market Economies (EMEs) are characterized by rapid economic growth, industrialization, and increasing integration into global trade and finance. Understanding the strength of financial capacity and absorption in these economies is crucial from a global economic perspective. The concept is rooted in finance-led growth hypotheses,

* **Corresponding author Sofia Devi Shamurailatpam:** Department of Banking and Insurance, Faculty of Commerce, The Maharaja Sayajirao University of Baroda, Vadodara, Gujarat, India;
E-mails: sofia.devi-bi@msubaroda.ac.in, sofeedevi@gmail.com

Mohammed Majeed, Sofia Devi Shamurailatpam, Parag Sunil Shukla, Ibrahim Osman & Hamidu Gafaru Dokurugu (Eds.)

whether demand-following or supply-leading, which highlight the importance of finance as a key driver of development (Ranis & Fei, 1961; Schumpeter, 1912). For emerging and developing market economies, finance is instrumental in achieving major economic goals and visions (Beck, Demirgüç-Kunt, & Levine, 2007).

In this context, it is essential to understand the state of financial inclusion and the extent to which finance reaches different segments of society, particularly in emerging market economies. Additionally, recognizing the sustainability of finance is critical for meeting sustainable development goals (UNDP, 2015). This chapter provides an overview of financial inclusion and sustainable finance in EMEs. While there is no universally accepted definition of EMEs, they are generally identified based on factors such as nominal GDP, demographic characteristics, contributions to global trade and finance, and relationships with international institutional investors, such as Foreign Institutional Investors (FII) or Foreign Direct Investment (FDI) (IMF, 2020). According to research by Duttagupta and Pazarbasioglu (2021), we have selected 20 emerging market countries that account for 34% of the world's GDP in nominal terms and 46% in purchasing power parity terms. These countries include: Argentina, Brazil, Chile, China, Colombia, Egypt, Hungary, India, Indonesia, Iran, Malaysia, Mexico, the Philippines, Poland, Russia, Saudi Arabia, South Africa, Thailand, Turkey, and the United Arab Emirates. These countries' structural changes present new challenges and opportunities for global integration and development strategies (World Bank, 2022).

One of the key sources of financial inclusion data is the World Bank's Global Findex database, which surveys around 150,000 households across 140 countries, providing insights into account holdings, credit and savings accounts, and methods of transferring funds for services or receiving government benefits (Demirgüç-Kunt *et al.*, 2018). This chapter draws on data from the World Bank's Global Findex, the IMF's Financial Access Survey, and macroeconomic indicators from the World Development Indicators (World Bank, 2022) to analyze financial inclusion in selected EMEs. The chapter is structured into six sections. Section II provides a brief review of the literature on financial inclusion in EMEs. Section III offers an overview of the state of financial inclusion in EMEs, based on World Bank and IMF data. The following section presents debates and discussions on the topic, while Section VI concludes the chapter.

A BRIEF REVIEW OF LITERATURE

Extensive literature exists regarding the issues of financial inclusion in Emerging Market Economies (EMEs), as financial inclusion is considered one of the major policy development goals nations aim to incorporate into achieving Sustainable Development Goals (SDGs). Over time, countries have made notable progress in financial inclusion and financial literacy programs, as evidenced by World Bank Surveys, the IMF Financial Access database, and various local, regional, and global surveys. Theoretically, there is a direct and positive linkage between financial inclusion and economic development (Beck *et al.*, 2007).

A study by Ozili (2022) found that financial inclusion is positively correlated with sustainable development, which was measured in terms of various economic, social, and environmental variables. The role of technology is also indispensable when considering growth models for countries. Khera *et al.* (2022) examined the role of technology in financial inclusion across 52 developing and emerging market economies. Their study revealed that the adoption of digital financial services has been a key driver of financial inclusion, with significant variations across countries and regions. African and Asian countries, in particular, have shown the greatest progress in financial inclusion. Innovations in financial services, such as mobile banking, have helped overcome infrastructural barriers and improved financial accessibility (Allen *et al.*, 2014). Allen and colleagues conducted a cross-country study of financial development and the financial inclusion gaps between African nations and other developing countries with similar levels of economic development, emphasizing how these innovations aid financial inclusion.

However, structural and institutional factors within economies may hinder financial inclusion in developing nations, leading to differences across countries, regions, and income levels (Barajas *et al.*, 2020). These findings support the conventional finance-led growth hypotheses, which suggest that a supply-leading or demand-following strategy should be implemented based on a region's structural and fundamental systems to stimulate economic growth (Levine, 2005). Hussain *et al.* (2024) found a significant positive long-term impact of financial inclusion on economic growth in Asia, with results being more pronounced in developing countries compared to developed countries. This highlights the positive association between economic progress and financial inclusion as a driving force behind shaping sustainable growth (Kapoor, 2014; Mushtaq & Bruneau, 2019; Abdul Karim *et al.*, 2022). These findings offer comprehensive policy insights for designing efficient and inclusive policies aimed at fostering sustainable economic growth in the region.

However, some studies argue that financial inclusion may negatively contribute to financial stability by accelerating credit growth, leading to an increase in non-performing loans, transaction costs, and exposure to risks associated with poor credit lines (Abubakari *et al.*, 2025; Igan & Pinheiro, 2011; Sahay *et al.*, 2015;

López & Winkler, 2019) or by creating vulnerabilities due to shadow banking and inadequate regulations (Isayev, 2024). These contrasting views highlight the varying implications of financial inclusion across regions and countries.

The role of regulators and policymakers is crucial in addressing existing gaps in accessibility, reducing barriers to financial services, and enhancing financial literacy in developing nations. Investment in network infrastructure, innovation in financial products and services designed for affordability, as well as the development of mobile money and fintech products, will play a vital role in promoting financial inclusion in emerging market economies.

AN OVERVIEW OF THE EXTENT OF FINANCIAL INCLUSION IN EMES

Emerging market economies are characterized by several fundamental features, including demographic structure, GDP per capita, trade, external debts, and capital formation (Duttagupta & Pazarbasioglu, 2021). As seen in Table **1**, these economies have made significant progress in their macroeconomic policies, reflected in rising per capita incomes, trade in services, and more than sixty percent of these countries following forward-looking inflation-targeting regimes that have contributed to stabilizing inflation (Duttagupta & Pazarbasioglu, 2021).

Other socio-economic and institutional factors also play a role in explaining the structure and development of these economies. Table **1** provides an overview of the macroeconomic variables of select EMEs, including total population by country, GDP per capita, gross capital formation, trade as a percentage of GDP, and external debt stocks as a percentage of GNI. According to the 2022 World Bank database, China and India each account for nearly 18 percent of the world's population, while countries like Brazil and Indonesia make up about 3 percent. The remaining 16 EMEs represent less than 1 percent of the world population.

These population sizes are reflected in GDP per capita figures, with India having a low GDP per capita of USD 2,098, compounded by a high Gini coefficient that indicates wealth inequality. Smaller countries like Hungary exhibit much higher GDP per capita at USD 16,345.31, and similarly, Poland, Saudi Arabia, and the UAE report significantly higher GDP per capita figures. In terms of gross capital formation as a percentage of GDP, China leads with over 40 percent, while countries like Iran, Hungary, Turkey, and India report capital formation rates above 30 percent, an important indicator for EMEs. The share of trade also supports this as a percentage of GDP, where EMEs outperform in exports and imports of goods and services.

Finally, data on external debt stocks as a percentage of GNI reflects the extent of countries' integration into the global economy through mutual agreements and the use of external borrowings.

Table 1. Macroeconomic indicators of emerging market economies, 2022.

Countries	Population, Total	(Population Total as % of World Population)	GDP per capita (constant 2015 US$)	Gross Capital formation (% of GDP)	Trade (% of GDP)	External Debt Stocks (% of GNI)
Argentina	46234830	(0.58%)	12940.74	17. 63	31.65	40.00
Brazil	215313498	(2.71%)	8822.05	18.01	38.81	31.11
Chile	19603733	(0.25%)	14235.36	25.59	74.99	--
China	1412175000	(17.76%)	11560.24	43.15	38.35	13.44
Colombia	51874024	(0.65%)	6836.23	19.74	48.07	55.79
Egypt	110990103	(1.40%)	4088.90	17.02	36.98	35.38
Hungary	9643048	(0.12%)	16345.31	33.97	185.27	--
India	1417173173	(17.82%)	2098.22	33.02	49.97	18.42
Indonesia	275501339	(3.46%)	4073.56	29.75	45.47	30.89
Iran	88550570	(1.11%)	5507.53	38.00	51.60	2.41
Malaysia	33938221	(0.43%)	11399.40	23.51	146.66	--
Mexico	127504125	(1.60%)	10078.60	22.70	88.45	41.92
Philippines	115559009	(1.45%)	3528.33	24.69	72.43	25.98
Poland	36821749	(0.46%)	17178.67	22.10	123.98	--
Russia	144236933	(1.81%)	10030.04	22.79	43.26	17.15
Saudi Arabia	36408820	(0.46%)	21478.82	26.43	63.51	--
South Africa	59893885	(0.75%)	6022.43	15.38	65.06	43.38
Thailand	71697030	(0.90%)	6275.93	27.83	132.86	39.95
Turkey	84979913	(1.07%)	14055.11	35.04	81.17	51.05
United Arab Emirates	9441129	(0.12%)	45698.01	22.79*	166.57*	--

*Data pertains to the year 2020.
Source: World Bank Database. (https://databank.worldbank.org/reports.aspx?source=2&country=ARE)

Understanding the structure of finance in emerging market economies (EMEs) is crucial, not only to assess the extent of outreach and accessibility but also for ensuring the sustainability of finance in meeting major policy goals. Table **2** presents key financial indicators for EMEs. Access to finance is the starting point for financial inclusion, followed by its usage, which is determined by the utility derived from using these financial products and services. These factors are successful in implementation when linked to financial development and finance-led growth hypotheses (Beck *et al.*, 2007). In other words, finance plays a critical role in providing or facilitating access to and usage of financial services at affordable costs, provided there is a solid economic infrastructure to support digitization processes.

Table **2** reports the progress of financial inclusion across 20 EMEs, based on World Bank surveys on financial inclusion, spanning from 2011 to 2021. There has been notable progress in various dimensions of financial accessibility in these countries. The number of adults with formal financial accounts, which was less than 50% in many countries, has reached nearly 95% in Poland and Thailand by 2021. Iran reported 90%, Brazil 84%, and China 89%, with 11 out of 20 EMEs having more than 80% of their populations opening accounts during this decade. These figures are indicative of positive progress in financial inclusion within these nations. Other countries also show gradual improvements in accessibility to finance, with more than 50% of the population opening accounts, except for Egypt, which stands at 27%.

Additionally, there has been significant progress in the use of mobile money accounts. Between 10% to 30% of the population in many countries have opted for digital methods of accessing finance, with Thailand achieving a notable 60%. The use of digital accounts is closely tied to mobile cellular subscriptions in these regions. The World Bank database shows that, in most EMEs, the number of mobile cellular subscriptions per 100 people has exceeded 100, with many individuals holding multiple subscriptions. However, countries like India, Brazil, and Egypt have lower rates of subscriptions per 100 people compared to other EMEs.

Table **3** illustrates the use of financial services in emerging market economies (EMEs) in terms of payments made or received, money stored or saved, borrowing from formal financial institutions (including credit cards), and households' ability to meet emergency financial requirements within a 30-day period. In Thailand, 83.4% of adults have received digital payments, followed by 75.2% in Hungary, 74.1% in Russia, and 71.9% in Chile. However, India has a much lower percentage, with only 19.4% of adults receiving digital payments in 2021, 17.9% in the UAE, and 16.5% in Egypt. Other EMEs have experienced digital payments received by between 40% and 60% of adults, according to the 2021 World Bank database.

Table 2. Financial accessibility in emerging market economies.

Countries	Account (% age 15+)				Mobile Money Account (% age 15+)		Mobile Cellular Subscriptions (per 100 people)
	2011	2014	2017	2021	2017	2021	2022
Argentina	33.1	50.2	48.7	71.6	2.4	35.1	132.36
Brazil	55.9	68.1	70.0	84.0	4.8	27.0	98.89
Chile	42.2	63.3	74.3	87.1	18.7	--	134.75
China	63.8	78.9	79.5	88.7	--	--	124.88
Colombia	30.4	39.0	45.8	59.7	4.7	21.8	155.79
Egypt	9.7	14.1	32.8	27.4	1.8	2.9	93.21
Hungary	72.7	72.3	74.9	88.2	--	--	104.06
India	35.2	53.1	79.9	77.5	2.0	10.4	80.65
Indonesia	19.6	36.1	48.9	51.8	3.1	9.3	114.90
Iran	73.7	92.3	94.0	90.0	26.3	12.4	164.50
Malaysia	66.2	80.7	85.3	88.4	10.9	28.0	141.29
Mexico	--	--	--	--	--	--	100.29
Philippines	26.6	31.3	34.5	51.4	4.5	21.7	144.04
Poland	70.2	77.9	86.7	95.7	--	--	131.94
Russia	48.2	67.4	75.8	89.7	--	32.9	168.98*
Saudi Arabia	46.4	69.4	71.7	74.3	--	--	132.38
South Africa	53.6	70.3	69.2	85.4	19.0	36.6	167.40
Thailand	72.7	78.1	81.6	95.6	8.3	60.0	176.32
Turkey	57.6	56.7	68.6	74.1	16.4	18.3	105.81
United Arab Emirates	59.7	83.7	88.2	85.7	21.3	13.3	212.22

Source: Klapper *et al.* (2022) & World Bank Database on World Development Indicators. (*, data pertains to 2021)

Table 3. Usage of financial services and products in EMEs, 2021.

Countries	Received a Digital Payment	Made a Digital Payment	Used an Account to store Money for Cash Management	Borrowed Formally, Including a Credit Card	Not Very Difficult to Access Emergency Money in 30 Days (All Adults)
Argentina	37.1	59.1	27.7	32.1	51.8
Brazil	49.8	70.7	38.3	41.3	45.2
Chile	71.9	77.6	55.8	24.2	57.4
China	52.3	84.5	60.4	39.2	83.7
Colombia	33.0	42.3	19.5	19.0	43.9
Egypt	16. 5	8.2	6.7	7.5	42.7
Hungary	75.2	81.4	75.2	18.9	75.0
India	19.4	24.7	34. 5	12.8	31.3
Indonesia	23.0	29.1	26.0	13.2	55.7
Iran	52.2	79.6	52.7	25.6	70.9
Malaysia	63.2	65.5	66.2	15.1	61.2
Mexico*	--	--	--	--	--
Philippines	28. 5	38. 5	24.9	18.8	50.3
Poland	66.6	91.4	77.1	31.9	81.7
Russia	74.1	82.4	56.0	30.8	73.8
Saudi Arabia	56.8	72.1	59.0	32.4	82.3
South Africa	66.0	70.5	58.0	19.0	39.9
Thailand	83.5	80.1	67.5	30.4	61.0
Turkey	46.6	61.7	25.0	38.0	41.1
United Arab Emirates	17.9	75.1	53.1	23.9	58.9

Source: Klapper *et al.* (2022). (*, data not available for 2021).

On the other hand, EMEs performed better in terms of payments made through digital platforms. Countries such as Poland, Hungary, China, and Thailand saw more than 65% of adults using accounts to store money for cash management. On average, 25% to 50% of adults in EMEs used accounts to store or save money for cash management in 2021. Regarding the use of financial products like borrowing money from formal financial sources, including credit cards, less than 40% of adults in EMEs borrowed funds.

The data on accessibility to funds during a short 30-day period indicate that many households are able to meet their financial requirements through various sources, with an average of 40% to a maximum of 84% in China. This suggests that EMEs are gradually transitioning towards greater accessibility and use of financial products and services in the digital age.

Thus, the accessibility and use of financial products and services in EMEs indicate steady progress toward financial inclusion. However, several barriers to inclusion remain, including geographical locations, regional structural features, infrastructural challenges (such as poor network facilities), lack of financial literacy, and inadequate legal and institutional frameworks in financial systems. These issues need to be addressed to overcome the exclusion of large populations. In this context, upgrading technological innovations in financial products and the delivery of services to unbanked and underserved areas will provide critical insights and directions toward achieving greater financial inclusion.

DEBATES AND DISCUSSIONS

The following propositions are pertinent to examine so far as the financial inclusion of emerging market economies is concerned:

a. **Financial Inclusion and Inclusive Growth:** The concept of financial inclusion entails the broadening of the financial system, offering better financial services and products with greater accessibility and outreach to the general population. This, in turn, is expected to improve the livelihood of individuals, alleviate poverty, and enhance the standard of living, especially for underserved segments of society, ultimately driving economic growth and development. The United Nations Sustainable Development Goals (SDGs) have integrated the role of finance in fostering inclusive growth and achieving key policy objectives in developing nations (UNDP, 2020). Numerous studies have confirmed the positive influence of financial inclusion on economic growth, indicating a linkage between financial depth and economic growth, as well as lower income inequality (Levine, 2005; Kim, 2016; Kim *et al.*, 2018; Van *et al.*, 2019; Hussain *et al.*, 2024). These findings suggest that enhanced financial inclusion fosters greater economic development. Conversely, conventional growth theories such as Solow (1956) argue that infusing more capital into the financial sector does not necessarily result in sustained growth, with economic growth eventually stagnating. Lucas (1988) similarly contended that financial sector development does not serve as a catalyst for economic growth. Hence, while financial inclusion and economic growth are often linked, the nature of their relationship is influenced not only by macroeconomic variables but also by institutional and structural factors in the economy, which can differ across countries (Beck *et al.*, 2000; Clarke *et al.*, 2006; Demirgüç-Kunt & Levine, 2009).

b. **Digitization and Financial Inclusion:** One of the primary barriers to financial inclusion identified in surveys across different regions is geographical location, particularly for underserved populations in remote areas. Banks and financial institutions have increasingly offered digital financial services to those excluded due to geographic constraints and poor infrastructure. Mobile phones and digital technology have played a key role in providing access to financial services, especially in regions where physical bank branches are scarce. The involvement of fintech in financial services delivery has made these services more accessible and convenient, bridging the gap for populations in hilly areas and remote islands. Digitization is also cost-effective, offering affordable and easily accessible services through mobile phones and retail agents, further promoting financial inclusion (Allen *et al.*, 2014). However, digital financial inclusion requires significant investments in both hard (network infrastructure) and soft (regulatory frameworks) aspects to cater to an ever-growing population using digital platforms. Moreover, concerns such as safety, security, fraud protection, financial crimes, and risks related to digital services need to be carefully managed by policymakers and regulators (Isayev, 2024).

c. **Financial Inclusion and Financial Stability:** A key aspect of financial inclusion in relation to national policy goals is its impact on financial stability. Studies have explored whether financial inclusion enhances or undermines financial stability. Providing affordable financial services, including microcredit, micro-insurance, and basic savings accounts, can increase access to finance for underserved populations. However, financial instability (*e.g.*, high Non-Performing Assets [NPAs], poor recovery mechanisms, or insufficient priority sector lending) can undermine the profitability and efficiency of financial institutions, thereby affecting the overall financial stability of an economy. Therefore, financial inclusion initiatives should complement the existing financial system, enhancing stability rather than acting as substitutes for current systems. For instance, prioritizing lending to sectors like agriculture, Small and Medium-sized Enterprises (SMEs), and handlooms requires well-structured regulatory mechanisms to ensure sustainable delivery (Hussain *et al.*, 2024). Failure to properly regulate financial inclusion may result in increased NPAs and declining productivity in the financial sector, ultimately harming financial stability (Sahay *et al.*, 2015).

d. **Financial Inclusion and Women Empowerment:** Financial inclusion plays a crucial role in empowering women and promoting gender equality. Microfinance in Bangladesh, for example, has been instrumental in empowering women, helping them escape poverty, engage in productive activities, and contribute to the broader economy. Financial inclusion provides women with the financial tools to build resilience against economic shocks, develop saving habits, and become more financially literate, which in turn leads to greater economic stability and equitable growth (Khera *et al.*, 2022). However, certain socio-cultural, religious, and psychological factors continue to pose significant barriers to financial inclusion for women in many societies. Therefore, it is essential to increase financial literacy and awareness, particularly through digitized platforms, to ensure that women, youth, and small entrepreneurs can fully participate in the financial system and contribute to inclusive economic growth (World Bank, 2020).

e. **Financial Inclusion and Sustainable Development:** Financial inclusion and sustainable development are inherently linked, with the former serving as an enabler of the latter. Financial inclusion supports the achievement of several SDGs by increasing access to financial services that promote poverty eradication, food security, gender equality, health, and well-being, among others (UNDP, 2020). By mobilizing savings and investments, financial inclusion contributes to capital formation, which enhances productivity and efficiency, thereby promoting inclusive growth and sustainable development (Jima & Makoni, 2023). Ultimately, by facilitating the flow of capital, financial inclusion helps create job opportunities, drive innovation, and reduce inequality, all of which are central goals of sustainable development.

Regional Heterogeneity in Financial Inclusion and Macroeconomic Outcomes

While aggregate statistics provide a broad overview of financial inclusion trends across Emerging Market Economies (EMEs), they often mask significant disparities both within and across regions. These intra-regional differences stem from varied historical, institutional, technological, and socio-cultural contexts. A nuanced exploration of these regional disparities is crucial for understanding why similar financial inclusion strategies produce different macroeconomic outcomes across countries.

Sub-Saharan Africa

In Sub-Saharan Africa, mobile money has become a dominant vehicle for financial inclusion. Kenya, through the M-Pesa platform, and Ghana, *via* MTN Mobile Money and other fintech innovations, have witnessed remarkable penetration of digital financial services, particularly in rural and underserved areas. These successes have been facilitated by supportive regulatory environments, strong telecom infrastructure, and high mobile phone penetration. In contrast, Nigeria—the continent's largest economy—lags in mobile money usage due to regulatory constraints, fragmented digital ecosystems, and trust deficits in the financial system. These differences significantly affect the macroeconomic benefits derived from financial inclusion. In Kenya and Ghana, enhanced access to finance has been linked to increased small-scale entrepreneurship, improved household savings, and greater resilience to economic shocks.

South and Southeast Asia

South Asia exhibits its own set of disparities. India, despite its flagship financial inclusion programs such as Pradhan Mantri Jan Dhan Yojana (PMJDY) and the proliferation of Aadhaar-linked bank accounts, continues to struggle with limited uptake of digital payments in rural areas. Barriers such as digital illiteracy, gender norms, and infrastructural deficits constrain the macroeconomic potential of inclusion efforts. On the other hand, Thailand presents a contrasting success story, where financial inclusion is buttressed by robust financial literacy campaigns, fintech innovation, and proactive central bank initiatives like the PromptPay system. As a result, Thailand has achieved a high level of digital payment adoption, which has contributed to formalizing its informal economy, increasing tax revenues, and promoting consumer spending.

Latin America

In Latin America, financial inclusion has been growing but remains uneven. Countries like Brazil have made notable progress through platforms such as PIX, a central bank-led instant payment system that has driven massive digital adoption. However, financial access in countries like Peru and Bolivia remains limited, particularly among indigenous populations and rural dwellers. Furthermore, structural issues such as income inequality, weak institutional trust, and inflation volatility in some economies reduce the efficacy of financial inclusion in fostering sustained macroeconomic improvements.

These regional variations illustrate that financial inclusion is not a one-size-fits-all solution. The success and macroeconomic impact of inclusion policies are contingent on complementary factors such as institutional quality, technological infrastructure, regulatory frameworks, and sociocultural dynamics. Hence, policy prescriptions must be context-specific and regionally sensitive.

Institutional Economics

Institutional economics posits that the quality of a country's institutions—its legal structures, governance mechanisms, property rights enforcement, and regulatory capacity—shapes the behavior and efficiency of its financial systems. In the context of financial inclusion, strong institutions ensure that financial products are accessible, reliable, and secure, thereby increasing user trust and participation.

Countries with robust institutional environments are more likely to channel financial inclusion into productive economic activities. For example, when property rights are well-protected, individuals and SMEs are more inclined to invest, borrow, and innovate using formal financial services. Conversely, in settings characterized by weak institutions, inclusion may be superficial—people may open accounts due to policy incentives, but actual usage remains low due to distrust or inefficiency in service delivery.

Therefore, financial inclusion should be viewed not merely as an outcome of financial sector expansion, but as a process embedded in and shaped by institutional quality. A theoretical model incorporating institutional variables—such as rule of law, regulatory quality, and corruption control—could offer a more nuanced understanding of how financial access translates into inclusive growth.

Schumpeterian Innovation Theory

Building on the work of Joseph Schumpeter, this framework emphasizes the centrality of innovation in driving economic growth, with finance playing a critical enabling role. According to Schumpeter, financial intermediaries facilitate economic development by reallocating resources toward innovative and entrepreneurial ventures. In emerging markets, where informal and micro-entrepreneurial activities dominate, financial inclusion can be the key to unlocking latent innovation potential.

Access to credit, insurance, and savings instruments enables individuals and businesses to manage risk, invest in new ideas, and adopt productivity-enhancing technologies. For example, the rise of fintech solutions in places like Indonesia and Colombia has supported digital entrepreneurship and boosted e-commerce, thus contributing to economic diversification and growth.

Integrating a Schumpeterian lens allows us to conceptualize financial inclusion not just as a welfare-enhancing tool but as a catalyst for structural transformation and innovation-led growth. Policymakers can then design inclusion strategies that prioritize innovation hubs, youth entrepreneurship, and SME financing as pathways to macroeconomic dynamism.

A Proposed Conceptual Model

To bridge these theoretical insights, a synthesized model is proposed. It links financial inclusion (measured through access, usage, and quality dimensions) to macroeconomic outcomes (*e.g.*, GDP growth, employment, income inequality) through mediating variables such as:

a. Institutional quality
b. Technological infrastructure
c. Entrepreneurial activity
d. Innovation uptake

This model would serve as a conceptual framework for empirical investigation, allowing researchers and policymakers to test context-specific hypotheses about the channels through which financial inclusion impacts economic development.

Theoretical Framework: Financial Inclusion and Macroeconomic Outcomes

1. Institutional Foundations (Institutional Economics)

Financial inclusion does not occur in a vacuum—it depends on the quality of formal institutions such as legal frameworks, property rights, financial regulation, and governance structures. According to North (1990), institutions are the "rules of the game" that shape economic behavior. The key idea is that strong institutions reduce transaction costs and information asymmetries, enabling broader financial participation.

2. Financial Infrastructure and Innovation (Schumpeterian Framework)

Building on Schumpeter's theory of economic development, financial inclusion fosters access to credit and savings, allowing entrepreneurs to invest in innovation. Financial development thus acts as an engine of creative destruction, reallocating resources toward more productive uses. The key idea is that financial inclusion supports entrepreneurship, innovation, and industrial upgrading—core drivers of Schumpeterian growth.

3. Digitization as a Transmission Mechanism

Digitization enhances the reach and efficiency of financial services, overcoming geographic, informational, and infrastructural barriers. This promotes inclusion in underserved regions and among marginalized populations. Digital platforms reduce costs and increase the scale of delivery, accelerating financial access and participation.

4. Aggregate Macroeconomic Outcomes

Financial inclusion—supported by sound institutions and digital infrastructure—leads to macroeconomic gains through: Increased aggregate savings and investment, Greater productivity and innovation, Enhanced consumption smoothing, Lower income inequality and Greater employment and economic resilience. See Table **4** below.

Table 4. Model summary.

Component	Role
Institutional Quality	Reduces barriers to access, builds trust in financial systems
Schumpeterian Finance	Enables innovation and entrepreneurial activity
Digitization	Overcomes spatial/transactional barriers, boosts participation
Macroeconomic Outcomes	Growth, inclusion, productivity, innovation, financial stability

Policy Relevance and SDG Alignment

Financial inclusion plays a pivotal role in achieving several Sustainable Development Goals (SDGs), particularly:

a. SDG 1 (No Poverty)
b. SDG 5 (Gender Equality)
c. SDG 8 (Decent Work and Economic Growth)
d. SDG 9 (Industry, Innovation and Infrastructure)
e. SDG 10 (Reduced Inequality)

According to Feyen, E *et al.* (2023), in the World Bank's *Global Findex Database*, financial inclusion fosters inclusive economic growth by enabling individuals to build savings, manage risk, and invest in education or enterprises, thus supporting poverty eradication and economic empowerment. Policymakers in emerging economies are increasingly embedding financial inclusion strategies into national development agendas as a pathway toward these global goals. Ozili (2018) emphasizes that financial inclusion should be approached not just as a banking or fintech agenda but as an enabler of social equity and sustainable development. In this view, macroeconomic policy tools (*e.g.*, targeted subsidies, financial literacy programs, regulatory reform) should be aligned with the broader SDG framework.

Digitization and Overcoming Geographic Barriers

One of the most transformative shifts in financial inclusion has been the role of digitization, particularly in overcoming spatial and infrastructural challenges in emerging markets.

a. Mobile Money and Agent Banking: Studies such as Jack & Suri (2014) on M-Pesa in Kenya show how mobile money platforms bypass the need for traditional bank branches, bringing financial services to rural and underserved populations. These tools are critical in addressing financial deserts – regions where formal banking is absent.
b. Fintech Ecosystems: According to UNCTAD (2020), fintech innovations – including mobile wallets, digital credit scoring, and peer-to-peer lending – are key drivers of financial deepening in remote areas. Governments have increasingly supported these ecosystems through regulatory sandboxes and digital identity frameworks.
c. Public-Private Partnerships (PPPs): Collaboration between central banks, telecom companies, and private fintechs has enabled low-cost, high-reach financial models. For example, in Ghana, the Mobile Money Interoperability platform allows seamless transactions between providers, reducing exclusion due to provider lock-in.
d. Geospatial Technologies & Infrastructure Mapping: Research by Chironga *et al.* (2017) highlights how data analytics and GIS mapping are used to locate underserved regions, allowing policymakers to target interventions more effectively and expand the financial footprint.

CONCLUSION

This chapter provides an overview of the state and progress of financial inclusion in emerging market economies (EMEs), drawing from country-level data on financial inclusion surveys and macroeconomic indicators sourced from the World Bank Group and the International Monetary Fund. Overall, EMEs have made significant strides under financial inclusion programs, which are complemented by financial literacy initiatives at the regional and local levels aimed at raising awareness of financial products and services, particularly in times of financial distress. From a macroeconomic perspective, financial inclusion in emerging economies must be viewed as a policy handle for inclusive growth and workable development. Aligning national strategies with the SDGs and leveraging digital transformation are critical for addressing geographic and socioeconomic inequalities. The success of such efforts depends not only on technology but on robust regulatory frameworks, infrastructure investments, and inclusive policies that ensure access, usage, and impact across all segments of the population. The process of digitization has accelerated the pace of financial inclusion across countries, driven by mobile network connectivity services that have extended financial access to remote and underserved areas. According to the World Bank Database surveys, there has been a notable increase in the accessibility of financial services, as indicated by the rising proportion of adults holding financial accounts. This progress is evident in various dimensions of financial inclusion, including savings behaviors, borrowing sources, and the confidence individuals have in managing financial distress or economic crises.

The rise of digital financial services has further promoted the use of electronic transactions. However, despite these advances, a segment of the population still relies on traditional banking systems and face-to-face services, which remain prevalent in certain regions. This highlights that while the digital transformation has been substantial, there remains a diverse range of preferences and needs when it comes to financial service delivery.

In summary, substantial progress has been made in terms of accessibility and utilization of financial products and services across EMEs. To ensure continued advancement, policymakers and regulatory bodies must address multiple facets of financial inclusion, including technology, gender equality, financial stability, inclusive growth, and sustainable development. By incorporating these diverse elements into a comprehensive and integrated financial inclusion framework, countries can build a more inclusive and resilient financial system that benefits all segments of society.

REFERENCES

Abdul Karim, Z., Nizam, R., Law, S.H., Hassan, M.K. (2022). Does financial inclusiveness affect economic growth? New evidence using a dynamic panel threshold regression. *Finance Research Letters, 46*(1), 102364.
[http://dx.doi.org/10.1016/j.frl.2021.102364]

Abubakari, A-R., Majeed, M., Alhassan, N., & Yomboi, J. (Eds). (2025). *Navigating the Fintech Frontier: Transformative Innovations and Risk Factors in Financial Services.* Sharjah (UAE): Bentham Science Publishers..
[http://dx.doi.org/10.2174/97898153249071250101]

Allen, F., Carletti, E., Cull, R., Qian, J., Senbet, L., & Valenzuela, P. (2014). African Financial development and financial inclusion gaps. *Journal of African Economies, 23*(5), 614–642. .

Asli, Demirgüç-Kunt, Ross, Levine (2009). Finance and Inequality: Theory and Evidence *Annual Review of Financial Economics, Annual Reviews, 1*(1), 287-318. Working Paper 15275 Available from: http://www.nber.org/papers/w15275

Ayyagari, M., Beck, T., Hoseini, M. (2021). *Finance in the digital age: Implications for inclusive growth. World Bank Policy Research Working Paper,* 9817.
[http://dx.doi.org/10.1596/1813-9450-9817]

Barajas, A., Beck, T., Belhaj, M., Naceur, S.B. (2020). Financial Inclusion: What have we learned so far? What do we have to learn? *IMF Working Paper WP/20/157,* 1-51.

[http://dx.doi.org/10.5089/9781513553009.001]

Beck, T., Levine, R., Loayza, N. (2000). Finance and the sources of growth. *Journal of Financial Economics, 58*(1-2), 261-300.
[http://dx.doi.org/10.1016/S0304-405X(00)00072-6]

Clarke, G.R.G., Xu, L.C., Zou, H. (2006). Finance and Income Inequality: What Do the Data Tell Us? *South Economic Associaton, 72*(3), 578-596.
[http://dx.doi.org/10.1002/j.2325-8012.2006.tb00721.x]

Chironga, M., De Grandis, H., Zouaoui, Y. (2017). *Mobile financial services in Africa: Winning the battle for the customer. McKinsey & Company.* Available from: https://www.mckinsey.com

Demirgüç-Kunt, A., Klapper, L., Singer, D., Ansar, S., & Hess, J. (2022). *The Global Findex Database 2021: Financial inclusion, digital payments, and resilience in the age of COVID-19.* Washington, DC: World Bank.
[http://dx.doi.org/10.1596/978-1-4648-1897-4]

Duttagupta, R., & Pazarbasioglu, C. (2021). Emerging markets must balance overcoming the pandemic, returning to more normal policies, and rebuilding their economies. *Finance and Development, 58*(2)..

Hussain, S., Rehman, A., Ullah, S., Waheed, A., & Hassan, S. (2024). Financial Inclusion and Economic Growth: Comparative Panel Evidence from Developed and Developing Asian Countries. *SAGE Open, 14*(1), 21582440241232585.
[http://dx.doi.org/10.1177/21582440241232585]

Igan, D., & Pinheiro, M. (2011). Credit growth and bank soundness: fast and furious? *IMF Work. Pap, 11*(278), 1.
[http://dx.doi.org/10.5089/9781463925956.001]

Isayev, M. (2024). Unraveling the interplay of financial inclusion, stability, and shadow banking in emerging markets. *Economic Change and Restructuring, 57*(2), 62.
[http://dx.doi.org/10.1007/s10644-024-09657-2]

Jack, W., Suri, T. (2014). Risk sharing and transactions costs: Evidence from Kenya's mobile money revolution. *American Economic Review, 104*(1), 183-223.
[http://dx.doi.org/10.1257/aer.104.1.183]

Kapoor, A. (2014). Financial inclusion and the future of the Indian economy. *Futures, 56*(1), 35-42.
[http://dx.doi.org/10.1016/j.futures.2013.10.007]

Kim, D. W., Yu, J. S., & Hassan, M. K. (2018). Financial inclusion and economic growth in OIC countries. *Research in International Business and Finance, 43*, 1-14.
[http://dx.doi.org/10.1016/j.ribaf.2017.07.178]

Kim, J.H. (2016). A study on the effect of financial inclusion on the relationship between income inequality and economic growth. *Emerging Markets Finance and Trade, 52*(2), 498-512.
[http://dx.doi.org/10.1080/1540496X.2016.1110467]

Klapper, L., Singer, D., & Ansar, S. (2022). *The little data book on financial inclusion 2022 volume 4.* World Bank Group. Available from: https://documents.worldbank.org/en/publication/documentsreports/documentdetail/099731410142211021/idu0bbc001f30973f04bf00a8db0909f3bff190a.

Khera, P., Ng, S., Ogawa, S., Sahay, R. (2022). Measuring Digital Financial Inclusion in Emerging Market and Developing Economies: A New Index. *Asian Economy Policy Review, 17*(2), 213-230.
[http://dx.doi.org/10.1111/aepr.12377]

Levine, R. (2005). Finance and growth: Theory and evidence. In: Aghion, P., Durlauf, S., (Eds.), *Handbook of economic growth.* Amsterdam, The Netherlands: Elsevier Science.
[http://dx.doi.org/10.1016/S1574-0684(05)01012-9]

López, T., Winkler, A. (2019). Does financial inclusion mitigate credit boom-bust cycles? *Journal of Financial Stability, 43*, 116-129.

[http://dx.doi.org/10.1016/j.jfs.2019.06.001]

Lucas, R.E., Jr (1988). On the mechanics of economic development. *Journal of Monetary Economics, 22*(1), 3-42.
[http://dx.doi.org/10.1016/0304-3932(88)90168-7]

Mushtaq, R., Bruneau, C. (2019). Microfinance, financial inclusion and ICT: Implications for poverty and inequality. *Technology in Society, 59*(2), 101154.
[http://dx.doi.org/10.1016/j.techsoc.2019.101154]

North, D.C. (1990). Institutions, institutional change and economic performance. *Cambridge University Press.*
[http://dx.doi.org/10.1017/CBO9780511808678]

Ozili, P.K. (2022). Financial inclusion and sustainable development: an empirical association. *Journal of Money and Business, 2*(2), 186-198.
[http://dx.doi.org/10.1108/JMB-03-2022-0019]

Ozili, P.K. (2018). Impact of digital finance on financial inclusion and stability. *Borsa Istanbul Review, 18*(4), 329-340.
[http://dx.doi.org/10.1016/j.bir.2017.12.003]

Sahay, M.R., Cihak, M., N'Diaye, M.P., Barajas, M.A., Mitra, M.S., Kyobe, M.A., Yousefi, M.R. (2015). Financial inclusion: can it meet multiple macroeconomic goals? *International Monetary Fund.*

Solow, R.M. (1956). A Contribution to the Theory of Economic Growth. *The Quarterly Journal of Economics, 70*(1), 65-94.
[http://dx.doi.org/10.2307/1884513]

Schumpeter, J.A. (1934). The theory of economic development: An inquiry into profits, capital, credit, interest, and the business cycle. *Harvard University Press.*

United Nations Conference on Trade and Development. (2021). *Financial inclusion for development: Better access to financial services for women, the poor, and micro, small and medium-sized enterprises.* Retrieved from https://unctad.org/webflyer/financial-inclusion-development.

Van, L.T.H., Vo, A.T., Nguyen, N.T., Vo, D.H. (2021). Financial Inclusion and Economic GROWTH: An International Evidence. *Emerging Markets Finance and Trade, 57*(1), 239-263.
[http://dx.doi.org/10.1080/1540496X.2019.1697672]

World Bank. (n.d.). World Development Indicators [Data set]. Retrieved November 6, 2025, from https://databank.worldbank.org/reports.aspx?source=2&country=ARE.

CHAPTER 2

The FinTech Journey: Bridging the Gaps in Financial Inclusion Through Artificial Intelligence

Aditya Keshari[1,*], **Upnishad Mishra**[2], **Milan Yadav**[3], **Pankaj Kumar**[4], **Kumari Neelam**[5] and **Umesh Gupta**[6]

[1] *Institute of Management, Nirma University, Ahmedabad, Gujarat, India*

[2] *School of Business, Galgotias University, Greater Noida, Uttar Pradesh, India*

[3] *School of Commerce, Galgotias University, Greater Noida, Uttar Pradesh, India*

[4] *Faculty of Commerce and Management, United University, Prayagraj, Uttar Pradesh, India*

[5] *Department of Commerce, Mahatma Gandhi Kashi Vidyapith University, Varanasi, Uttar Pradesh, India*

[6] *School of Business and Management Studies, MATS University, Raipur, Chhattisgarh, India*

Abstract: This chapter begins with a historical overview of Artificial Intelligence (AI), tracing its conceptual origins and examining its evolution as a transformative force in the financial sector. AI has emerged as a powerful tool in enhancing financial inclusion, particularly in improving accessibility to financial services for marginalized and underserved communities. Financial inclusion, defined as universal access to affordable financial services, is critical for poverty reduction and overall economic development. However, despite significant progress, billions of people worldwide remain unbanked or underbanked. The chapter explores how Artificial Intelligence and Financial Technology (FinTech) are addressing these challenges by creating new opportunities for financial access through innovative digital solutions. Key FinTech innovations such as mobile banking, Peer-to-Peer (P2P) lending, blockchain technology, and digital wallets are helping to break down traditional barriers to financial services by offering affordable, accessible, and user-centric alternatives to conventional banking systems. AI plays a pivotal role in enhancing these innovations by automating critical processes such as Know Your Customer (KYC) and Anti-Money Laundering (AML) procedures, thereby simplifying compliance and reducing costs. Additionally, AI improves fraud detection and contributes to the creation of personalized financial experiences through data-driven insights, tailoring services to meet the unique needs of individual users. The chapter concludes by exploring the potential of FinTech and AI to foster a more equitable financial landscape. By adopting responsible and inclusive approaches to these technologies, there is significant potential to achieve greater financial inclusion , particularly in emerging markets. When

* **Corresponding author Aditya Keshari:** Institute of Management, Nirma University, Ahmedabad, Gujarat, India; E-mail: adityakeshari@fmsbhu.ac.in

Mohammed Majeed, Sofia Devi Shamurailatpam, Parag Sunil Shukla, Ibrahim Osman & Hamidu Gafaru Dokurugu (Eds.)

deployed thoughtfully, these technologies can not only address the challenges of financial access but also catalyze sustainable economic growth and development.

Keywords: Artificial super intelligence, Artificial intelligence, Financial inclusion, FinTech.

INTRODUCTION

The evolution of Financial Technology (FinTech) is closely linked to the advancement of Artificial Intelligence (AI), a discipline initiated by trailblazers such as Alan Turing, Marvin Minsky, and John McCarthy. The following passage beautifully highlights the transformative role AI is playing in the FinTech sector, especially in terms of improving financial inclusion. The application of AI in FinTech is indeed opening up new possibilities, particularly for the unbanked and underbanked populations who have historically faced barriers to accessing essential financial services.

The idea that AI can tackle financial inclusion gaps by enabling mobile banking, peer-to-peer lending, and blockchain technology is critical. These innovations create a more accessible and efficient ecosystem, allowing individuals in rural or remote areas to bypass traditional financial infrastructure and engage in the global economy. AI also supports these services by improving security, providing predictive analytics, and creating personalized financial experiences for users, which is especially important for fostering trust in new technologies.

Additionally, the ability of AI to assist in fraud prevention and regulatory compliance is particularly relevant. AI algorithms can monitor transactions in real-time, detect anomalies, and ensure that financial institutions remain in compliance with evolving regulations. This proactive approach helps prevent financial crime while promoting a safer environment for users to engage with financial systems.

By focusing on these points, the chapter provides an insightful look into the convergence of AI and FinTech, which is reshaping the financial landscape and offering opportunities for economic empowerment. It will be interesting to explore specific case studies of how AI has already made an impact in financial inclusion efforts and the lessons learned from these early applications. This chapter elucidates the connections between AI and FinTech in the continuous pursuit of financial inclusion.

THEORETICAL BACKGROUND

Artificial Intelligence

This passage provides a rich historical overview of the development and various definitions of Artificial Intelligence (AI), tracing its origins from Turing's groundbreaking work to contemporary perspectives. The inclusion of Turing's questions about whether machines can think and whether they could perform well in the imitation game sets the stage for the evolution of AI. The idea of a machine mimicking human-like intelligence, central to Turing's concept, still resonates with modern AI approaches, where the focus is often on creating systems that can simulate cognitive functions. The Turing Test, introduced in 1950, remains one of the most iconic benchmarks for AI to this day.

Marvin Minsky's development of the SNARC neural network in 1951 is another pivotal moment, as it marks the first attempt to model a machine after the human brain's structure, introducing the concept of artificial neural networks. Minsky's work laid the groundwork for the field of machine learning, which has seen a resurgence in recent decades.

John McCarthy's coining of the term "Artificial Intelligence" at the Dartmouth Conference in 1956 is also a milestone in AI history. His definition, alongside others like those of Marvin Minsky and Nils J. Nilsson, reflects a broad understanding of AI that focuses on simulating human-like intelligence and behaviors. These definitions underscore AI's goal of making machines act intelligently, often in a way that mirrors human cognitive abilities such as reasoning, learning, and problem-solving. The definitions provided by Castro and New (2016) and Rao (2017) emphasize the wide range of capabilities that AI can possess, from interacting with humans and machines to perceiving and responding to its environment. These functions highlight AI's role as not just a tool for computational tasks, but a versatile technology with the potential to perform complex tasks that would otherwise require human intelligence.

The quote from Jean-Paul Simon (2019) points out the diversity of opinions in the AI community, which is not surprising given the complexity of defining intelligence itself. There is no single, universally accepted definition of AI, which can vary depending on the perspective or application, reflecting the interdisciplinary nature of the field. This historical context provides an understanding of the evolution of AI from its conceptual beginnings to its current state as a powerful tool impacting many aspects of modern life. The development of AI continues to be shaped by ongoing debates around its definitions, goals, and ethical implications.

Different Stages of AI

The three stages of AI in more detail:

1. **Artificial Narrow Intelligence (ANI)**: ANI is the most common form of AI today. It refers to machines that are highly specialized and can perform a specific task, but their intelligence is limited to that task. Siri, for example, is a classic example of ANI. It can recognize voice commands, provide responses, set reminders, and perform other predefined tasks, but it lacks the ability to understand or perform beyond the specific tasks it was designed for. ANI systems operate with a narrow focus and do not have self-awareness, general reasoning abilities, or creativity in the way humans do.
2. **Artificial General Intelligence (AGI)**: AGI, also known as "strong AI," is the hypothetical level of AI that can perform any intellectual task that a human can do. Unlike ANI, which is limited to specific functions, AGI would have the capacity for general reasoning, problem-solving, learning, and adapting across a wide range of tasks. It would not only be able to perform multiple functions but would also exhibit a level of awareness, common sense, and contextual understanding similar to human cognition. However, AGI is still a long-term goal in the field of AI and has not been realized as of now.
3. **Artificial Superintelligence (ASI)**: ASI refers to a level of AI that surpasses human intelligence in virtually all aspects, including problem-solving, creativity, and emotional understanding. It would not only be able to perform every task a human can do but would also be capable of vastly outperforming human intelligence in virtually every domain. ASI could potentially alter its own architecture and improve upon itself, making it incredibly powerful and unpredictable. While it remains a theoretical concept, discussions about ASI raise significant concerns regarding safety, ethics, and control.

Example of Apple's Siri

Siri is a good example of ANI, as it's designed to handle a set range of tasks—such as answering questions, setting alarms, and sending messages—through voice recognition and processing. While Siri appears intelligent, it is a narrow, predefined system with no true understanding or consciousness behind its actions. To visualize the progression of these stages, we can consider a figure that might illustrate how Siri, at the ANI level, is very much specialized for a narrow set of functions, while AGI and ASI would show systems that adapt, learn, and evolve to handle a wider range of tasks and even exceed human performance in specific areas (Fig. **1**).

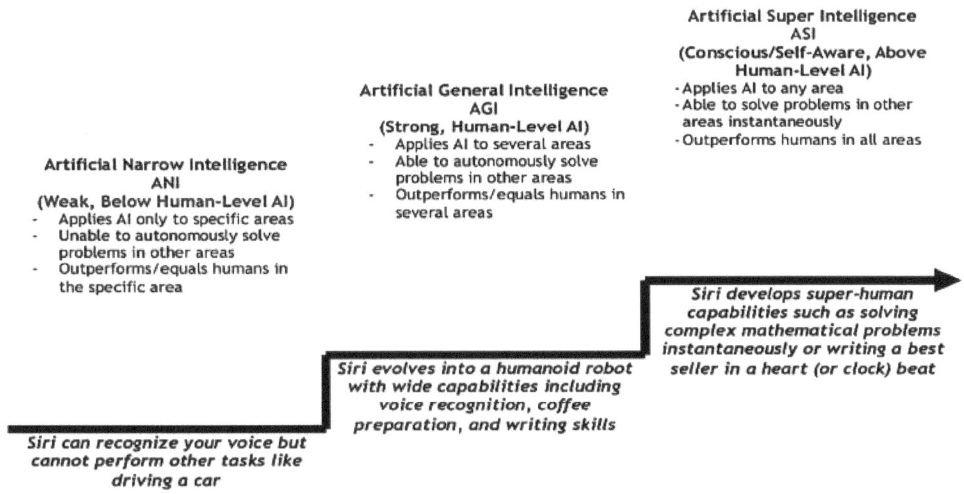

Fig. (1). Different stages of AI.
Source: (Kaplan and Haenlein 2018).

Financial Inclusion

Financial inclusion encompasses the accessibility and utilization of formal financial services by individuals and businesses. Policymakers view it as a means to enhance living standards, alleviate poverty, and stimulate economic development (IMF, 2015). Another perspective defines financial inclusion as the ability to obtain and employ financial services tailored to users' needs (BIS, 2015). Essentially, financial inclusion entails universal access to affordable financial services provided by credible and enduring institutions. This concept encompasses lending, insurance, investment, and savings. The market for the financially underserved includes those typically categorized as unbanked and underbanked. Despite significant progress in basic account ownership for individuals to promote financial inclusion, billions of people in both developed and developing nations remain financially underserved. Globally, over two billion individuals lack access to fundamental financial services and are unbanked. Additionally, several billion people with basic accounts are underserved by the financial sector, lacking access to credit, insurancc, or savings options.

Financial exclusion is characterized as the processes that prevent certain socioeconomic groups and individuals from accessing the formal financial system (Leyshon & Thrift, 1996). According to Sinclair (2001), financial exclusion is the inability to access necessary financial services in an appropriate manner. Carbó *et al.* (2005) define financial exclusion as the inability of certain social groups to utilize the financial system.

The potential of financial inclusion to revolutionize Micro and Small Enterprises (MSEs) and individuals is significant. Historically, financial institutions have overlooked low-income people, women, and other socioeconomically marginalized groups. Due to their inability to access professional services and products, as well as a lack of adaptability and know-how, these groups have often turned to informal, unregulated financial tools (Fig. **2**). Previous research indicates that financial services can enable individuals and businesses to thrive by leveraging economic opportunities and enhancing resilience. Additionally, these services can help people and organizations prepare for, withstand, or bounce back from unforeseen events such as sudden medical costs or weather-related disasters linked to climate change.

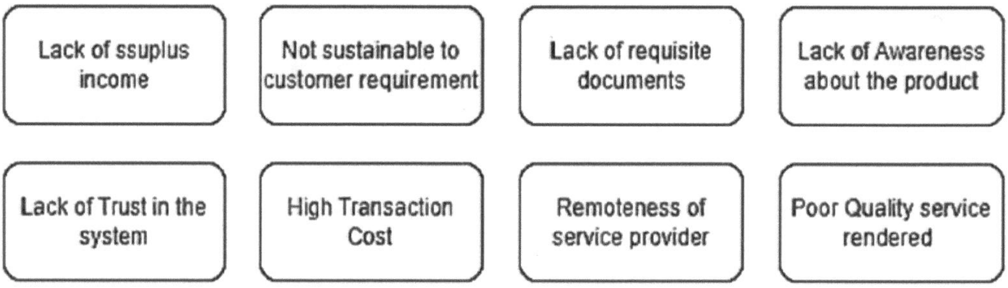

Fig. (2). Causes of financial exclusion.
Source: Authors' Own Creation.

Financial Inclusion and United Nations Sustainable Development Goals

Understanding financial inclusion is essential, as it plays a vital role in the global effort to achieve sustainable development. By enhancing the lives of disadvantaged and marginalized populations, financial inclusion aligns with seven of the seventeen United Nation's Sustainable Development Goals (SDGs) for 2030 (Fig. **3**). Sustainable Development Goals, 2018. (Home). Research by Danladi *et al.* (2023) indicates that developing nations are investigating cooperative strategies for Fintech adoption to attain the SDGs through financial inclusion. Their research highlights the importance of collaborations among diverse stakeholders, including governments, businesses, and non-profit organizations, to boost the utilization and effectiveness of Fintech in promoting financial inclusion. The authors contend that such partnerships are essential for surmounting obstacles to financial inclusion and realizing sustainable development objectives.

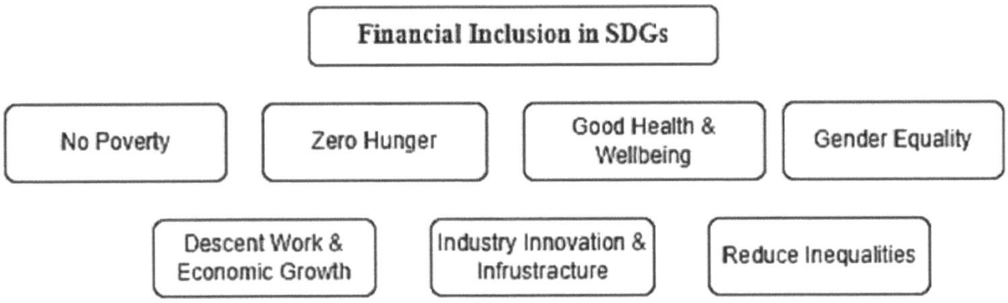

Fig. (3). Financial inclusion in SDGs.
Source: UNSGSA (2018).

Defining Financial Inclusion in the Indian Context

Financial inclusion is described as "The process of ensuring that vulnerable groups, including low-income and disadvantaged segments, have timely and adequate access to financial services at a reasonable cost." Dr. C. Rangarajan chaired the RBI's Committee on Financial Inclusion in 2008. In 2015, the Committee on Medium-term path to Financial Inclusion, led by Shri Deepak Mohanty of the RBI, outlined a vision for financial inclusion. This vision encompasses "easy access to a range of essential formal financial products and services, including credit, savings, remittance, government-sponsored insurance, and pension products for low-income households and small and marginal farmers at affordable prices with adequate protection, gradually enhanced by social cash transactions." To gain a deeper understanding of financial inclusion, the components of financial inclusion strategies and the regulation of financial inclusion in India are presented in Table **1**.

Table 1. Elements of financial inclusion strategies.

Strategy	Description/Examples
Inclusive Financial Institutions	-**Regional Rural Banks (RRBs)**: Banks focusing on rural populations. -**United Community Banks**: Community-focused banks serving local needs. -**Local Area Banks**: Banks catering to specific geographic regions. -**NBFC-MFIs (Non-Banking Financial Companies – Microfinance Institutions)**: Provide microloans to underserved populations, especially in rural and low-income areas.
Subsidized Funding	-**Micro Units Development and Refinance Agency Bank (MUDRA)**: Provides refinancing and support to micro-enterprises, helping small businesses access affordable credit.
Innovative Financial Products and Services	-**No-frills Bank Accounts**: Basic bank accounts with minimal charges, aimed at low-income and rural populations. -**Business Correspondents**: Intermediaries that provide banking services to underserved populations, especially in remote areas.

(Table 1) cont.....

Strategy	Description/Examples
Innovative Delivery Technologies	-**Telephone Bill-Paying Services**: Using phones (mobile or landline) to conduct financial transactions like bill payments and fund transfers, especially in rural areas.
To Enhance Credit Access	-**Credit Bureaus**: Provide credit information to help financial institutions assess lending risk and expand credit access. -**Stock-Exchange Platforms for Small and Medium-sized Businesses**: Allow SMBs to access capital by listing on exchanges or alternative platforms, providing access to funding.

Source: Authors' Own creation.

Financial Inclusion Strategies

These strategies work together to create a more inclusive financial ecosystem. By improving access to financial services and products, and by using innovative delivery methods like mobile banking and community-based services, these strategies help break down the barriers that prevent people from participating in the formal financial system. The ultimate goal is to ensure that individuals and businesses—particularly those in rural and underserved areas—can take advantage of financial services that empower them to improve their quality of life, grow their businesses, and contribute to the broader economy. It is summarized in Table **1**:

1. Inclusive Financial Institutions:

Regional Rural Banks (RRBs): These banks serve rural areas, where financial services are typically less accessible. By focusing on underserved rural populations, RRBs play a critical role in broadening access to financial products like savings accounts, loans, and insurance.

United Community Banks: These community-focused banks are designed to meet the specific needs of local populations, fostering trust and improving access to capital for small businesses and individuals.

Local Area Banks: These banks cater to specific geographic regions and smaller communities, providing financial products that are tailored to local needs and challenges.

NBFC-MFIs (Non-Banking Financial Companies – Microfinance Institutions): These institutions are dedicated to providing microloans to individuals, particularly in rural and low-income areas. They focus on financial inclusion by offering small loans for entrepreneurs and individuals who may not be able to access traditional banking services.

2. Subsidized Funding:

Micro Units Development and Refinance Agency Bank (MUDRA): MUDRA Bank was set up by the Indian government to provide refinancing and support to micro-enterprises. It facilitates access to affordable credit for small businesses, enabling them to grow and create jobs. Through subsidized funding programs, MUDRA ensures that even the smallest businesses can access financial resources to fuel their operations.

3. Innovative Financial Products and Services:

No-frills Bank Accounts: These are basic bank accounts with minimal charges, often targeting low-income and rural populations who might not have access to more traditional banking services. They are designed to provide access to a simple and affordable way to deposit money and make basic financial transactions. These accounts can be upgraded over time to offer additional services like credit and insurance products.

Business Correspondents: These are individuals or entities that act as intermediaries between the bank and customers, especially in rural areas. They facilitate banking services such as deposits, withdrawals, and loan applications, bridging the gap for people who may live far from traditional bank branches.

4. Innovative Delivery Technologies:

Telephone Bill-Paying Services: Using mobile phones or landlines for financial transactions has become an effective way to reach remote populations. In areas where people have limited access to bank branches, telephone bill-paying services offer a simple way to conduct transactions like bill payments, fund transfers, and access to basic banking services. This can be especially helpful for rural customers who may have limited access to the internet but can still access financial services via phone.

5. To Enhance Credit Access:

Credit Bureaus: Credit bureaus are key to improving access to credit, especially for people who don't have traditional credit histories. By collecting and providing information about individuals' borrowing and repayment behaviors, credit bureaus help financial institutions assess risk and make informed lending decisions. This can help expand credit access to previously underserved populations, such as those in rural or low-income areas.

Stock-exchange Platforms for Small and Medium-sized Businesses (SMBs): These platforms allow small businesses to access capital by listing on the stock exchange or through other investment channels. These businesses often face barriers to financing through traditional means, and stock-exchange platforms provide an alternative route for raising funds. This can be crucial for the growth and sustainability of SMBs, enabling them to expand and hire more workers.

Financial Inclusion Index of India FY 2020-2024

The Reserve Bank of India (RBI) developed the Financial Inclusion Index (FI-Index) to assess the extent of access to financial services across the country. Introduced in 2021, the FI-Index is published annually every July. The index is measured on a scale from 0 to 100, where 100 signifies complete financial inclusion and 0 represents total financial exclusion (refer to Table **2** below). According to the RBI, the financial inclusion index for India stood at 64.2 for the fiscal year 2023–24, reflecting a significant improvement from 53.9 in 2020–21. This increase highlights progress in making financial services more accessible. The index tracks access to and usage of formal financial services, including banking, insurance, investments, pensions, and postal services.

Table 2. Findings of the financial inclusion index over.

Financial Year	Index Value
2020-21	53.9
2021-22	56.4
2022-23	60.1
2023-24	64.2

Source: Reserve Bank of India (2024).

Elements of Financial Inclusion

The degree of financial inclusion for a household is shaped by six key components, as illustrated in Fig. (**4**) below. One of the central elements is financial literacy, which primarily focuses on education, although training and skill development may also be incorporated. Financial literacy has become a core component of national financial inclusion strategies in many countries (OECD, 2015). It is argued that to protect historically underserved and neglected groups from exploitative practices within the financial sector, these groups must be educated on how to access and use financial services. However, empirical evidence linking financial education directly to changes in household financial outcomes or behavior remains scarce (Lyons *et al.*, 2006; Lyons & Scherpf, 2004).

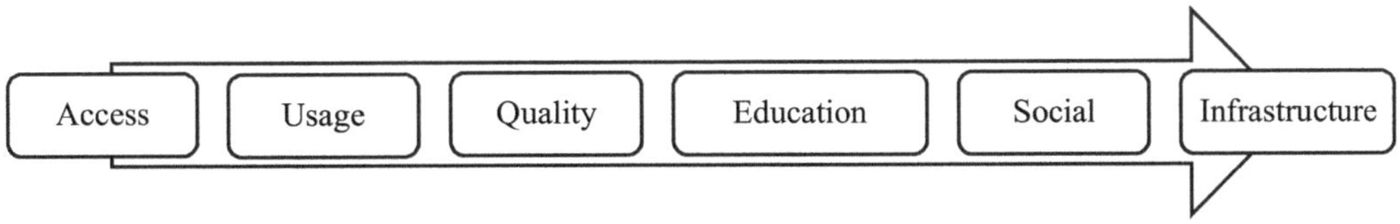

Fig. (4). Elements of financial inclusion.
Source: Lyons *et al.* (2017).

Additional factors are necessary to create an environment where individuals can effectively apply and practice financial knowledge. For example, social factors-such as a household's network of family, friends, neighbors, and the community—can provide vital social capital or social insurance. These networks help individuals decide whether or not to engage in formal financial markets. Households with weaker social support structures often struggle to apply financial knowledge in practical ways (Lyons *et al.*, 2017).

Furthermore, infrastructure and technological factors present significant barriers to financial inclusion. The lack of infrastructure, such as smartphones, Point of Sale (POS) terminals, banking agents, mobile towers, and internet connectivity, complicates access to financial services in many regions (Asian Development Bank, 2017; Lyons *et al.*, 2017). These challenges prevent financial inclusion from becoming a reality in areas where the necessary technology and infrastructure are absent (Jennah, 2017; Lyons *et al.*, 2017; Villasenor *et al.*, 2016). International organizations have concluded that, in order for financial inclusion to effectively influence behavior, national financial inclusion agendas and strategies must integrate not only access, usage, and quality, but also these other critical dimensions (Group, 2015; Lyons *et al.*, 2017; Sahay *et al.*, 2015).

AI HELPING THE FINTECH INDUSTRY

In the fintech industry, Artificial Intelligence (AI) has emerged as a transformative force, driving a wave of innovation, efficiency, and personalized services within financial institutions. Both fintech startups and traditional financial organizations are increasingly leveraging AI to enhance decision-making, automate complex tasks, and deliver highly personalized offerings that were previously unimaginable. By enabling the analysis of large volumes of data, AI helps financial firms derive valuable insights and streamline their operations, creating significant improvements across various sectors.

Unlike traditional algorithms that follow fixed, predefined rules, AI systems are designed to learn from data and adapt over time, improving their performance as they process more information. This flexibility makes AI particularly suited to the fast-paced, data-driven nature of financial services, where both market conditions and consumer needs are constantly evolving. As the demand for digital banking, mobile payments, and online financial services has surged, so has the adoption of AI, as businesses seek to maintain a competitive edge through cutting-edge technology.

One of the notable applications of AI in fintech is Natural Language Processing (NLP), which enables systems to understand and respond to customer inquiries in real time. By processing requests quickly and accurately, AI minimizes the need for human intervention, leading to reduced operational costs and enhanced customer satisfaction. Additionally, AI allows for the creation of truly personalized solutions by tailoring services to individual customer preferences and financial behaviors.

Beyond improving customer experiences, AI is revolutionizing core financial processes. In areas such as risk assessment, credit scoring, fraud detection, and regulatory compliance, AI is enhancing accuracy and efficiency. By analyzing complex patterns across large datasets, AI can identify potential risks, uncover fraudulent activities, and ensure compliance with regulations at an unprecedented speed, helping financial institutions operate more securely and effectively. In summary, AI is reshaping the fintech landscape by optimizing operations, offering personalized services, and improving critical financial processes, making it an indispensable tool for the industry's continued growth and transformation.

APPLICATION OF AI IN FINTECH

Artificial Intelligence (AI) has played a transformative role in revolutionizing numerous aspects of the financial services industry, enhancing productivity, accuracy, and user experience. One of the most significant applications of AI is in fraud detection and prevention. By analyzing vast amounts of transaction data in real time, AI can identify unusual behaviors and flag potentially fraudulent activity. Unlike traditional fraud detection methods, which rely on fixed rules, AI continuously learns and adapts to emerging patterns, providing a dynamic and proactive approach to risk management. Through the construction of predictive models based on historical fraud cases, AI not only detects fraud as it occurs but also forecasts potential future fraud risks, drastically reducing losses.

AI is also transforming credit rating and risk assessment procedures. Traditional credit scoring models primarily rely on past credit history, overlooking important factors for individuals with limited or no credit records. AI, however, can incorporate additional data sources—such as transactional behaviors, spending patterns, social media activity, and utility payment histories—to build a more comprehensive picture of a person's financial habits. This results in more accurate predictions of default risk and allows financial institutions to serve a broader, more inclusive clientele, including those who are underbanked. As AI models improve through continuous learning, lending decisions become faster, more equitable, and more inclusive.

In algorithmic and automated trading, AI has reshaped how financial assets are bought and sold. AI-powered algorithms can quickly analyze vast amounts of data, including historical prices, financial news, and economic indicators, to spot and capitalize on trading opportunities faster than human traders. These algorithms play a key role in High-Frequency Trading (HFT), where transactions are executed in milliseconds, making decisions based on current market conditions. AI also enables sentiment analysis by scanning social media, news outlets, and financial reports to gauge market sentiment. By considering public opinion, AI systems help traders predict market fluctuations and adjust their strategies in real-time.

In customer support, AI-driven chatbots and virtual assistants have revolutionized how financial institutions engage with their clients. Powered by Natural Language Processing (NLP), these AI systems provide round-the-clock customer service, drastically reducing wait times and overhead costs compared to human agents. AI chatbots can manage large volumes of inquiries simultaneously, offering prompt responses and guiding users through processes. Moreover, these virtual assistants enhance customer engagement and retention by delivering personalized financial advice based on user data, making them valuable tools for financial institutions.

AI also plays a pivotal role in personalized financial management. Fintech apps leverage AI to help users manage their finances by analyzing spending patterns, income trends, and savings goals to provide customized budgeting and investment recommendations. Robo-advisors, which offer automated portfolio management services, use AI to tailor investment strategies to an individual's financial goals. These AI-powered tools make investing more accessible and affordable, especially for people who may not have the resources or knowledge to consult traditional financial advisors. Robo-advisors adjust portfolios in real time based on user preferences and market conditions, offering services at a fraction of the cost of human financial advisors.

Another area where AI is making a significant impact is RegTech—the use of AI to ensure regulatory compliance. Financial institutions must adhere to regulations such as Know Your Customer (KYC) and Anti-Money Laundering (AML) laws, but compliance can be time-consuming and costly. AI automates the analysis of large datasets, allowing for real-time monitoring of transactions and customer behavior to ensure compliance. By detecting suspicious patterns indicative of money laundering or other illicit activities, AI helps financial institutions avoid regulatory penalties and ensures the accuracy and efficiency of compliance processes.

In summary, AI is playing an increasingly crucial role in fintech, driving advancements across many areas, including fraud detection, credit scoring, trading, customer service, personalized financial management, and regulatory compliance. As AI technology continues to evolve, its applications in the financial services sector will only expand, providing faster, more secure, and more personalized services to clients. These innovations are reshaping the financial landscape, making financial services more responsive, efficient, and accessible to meet the diverse needs of both the market and individual customers.

FINTECH EMPOWERING THE UNBANKED THROUGH FINANCIAL INCLUSION

In India's ongoing digital revolution, fintech is playing a pivotal role in driving technical advancements that are essential for the nation's economic growth. The financial sector has increasingly been shaped by fintech, which leverages innovative technologies to enhance and compete with traditional methods of delivering financial services, particularly through digital and mobile platforms. As one of the world's fastest-growing economies, India is a key destination for foreign investments across various industries. However, financial inclusion cannot be achieved unless everyone has access to a broader range of banking services. Moreover, the Government of India's ambitious "Digital India" initiative, aimed at empowering every citizen digitally, cannot succeed by merely expanding financial services. The initiative seeks to strengthen India's IT leadership and improve essential sectors such as banking, education, and healthcare (Deb & Agrawal, 2017).

Over the last decade, the Indian government's push for digitalization has gained significant momentum, attracting both private citizens and businesses. A large proportion of India's population resides in rural and semi-urban areas, where the key goal for economic growth is improving financial inclusion, particularly for the unbanked and underbanked. Credit accessibility plays a crucial role in achieving this goal. The absence of basic banking services, lack of credit histories, and lengthy loan application processes have made it challenging for Micro, Small, and Medium Enterprises (MSMEs) and the majority of the population in Tier-2 cities to access timely credit through formal channels.

As per Section 5(b) of the Banking Regulation (BR) Act of 1949, the core activities of a banking company include lending money, whether conducted online or offline. To engage in digital lending, all banks, including public and private sector banks, cooperative banks, small finance banks, and regional rural banks, must be registered with the Reserve Bank of India (RBI). Additionally, under the RBI Act of 1934, Non-Banking Financial Companies (NBFCs) that meet certain criteria must also register with the RBI to engage in financial services.

FINTECH INNOVATIONS: A GAME-CHANGER FOR THE UNBANKED

Fintech solutions leverage digital technology to deliver advanced financial services outside of traditional banking frameworks. These innovations present a unique opportunity for the unbanked to overcome challenges such as geographical limitations, high fees, and the complex documentation often required by conventional banks. In recent years, Indian fintech companies have been at the forefront of transforming the financial services sector. By utilizing digital platforms, mobile technologies, and innovative business models, these companies are democratizing access to financial services and empowering the unbanked.

Research by Goswami *et al.* (2022) examines the impact of fintech on financial inclusion in rural India, focusing on the substantial increase in the availability of financial products to underserved communities through digital financial services. Their findings emphasize how fintech's ability to offer affordable and accessible financial solutions can significantly bridge the financial inclusion gap in rural areas.

Digital banking applications have revolutionized the financial sector by enabling users to manage accounts, access financial information, and conduct transactions electronically. This is particularly beneficial in regions lacking traditional banking infrastructure (Gomber *et al.*, 2018). Fintech spans a broad array of products and services, such as peer-to-peer lending, blockchain technology, mobile banking, digital payments, and Artificial Intelligence (AI). By enhancing efficiency, accessibility, and convenience, these technologies have the potential to make financial services more valuable and available to a larger population (Gomber *et al.*, 2018). Fintech is poised to improve financial inclusion significantly, offering affordable financial services to underserved or unbanked populations, thereby driving economic growth and reducing poverty (Arner *et al.*, 2018).

Mobile Banking and Digital Wallets

Digital wallets and mobile banking are among the most significant fintech innovations for promoting financial inclusion, especially for the unbanked. Given the widespread availability of smartphones, even in remote areas, people can now access essential banking services through mobile apps. These applications enable users to obtain credit, store money, and make payments, even without a traditional bank account. Mobile money has proven to be a powerful tool for financial inclusion in India. Platforms such as PhonePe, Amazon Pay, BHIM, and Yono

SBI allow users to transfer and receive money, pay bills, and access other financial services directly through their mobile phones.

Mobile money providers are bridging the gap for millions of Indians, including those in rural areas, by establishing an extensive network of agents and merchants across the country. Fintech has not only revolutionized payment methods but also facilitated cashless transactions through electronic platforms like digital wallets, payment applications, and online payment gateways (Golubev & Ryabov, 2020). These innovations are providing greater financial accessibility to previously underserved populations, significantly advancing financial inclusion in India.

Peer-to-Peer Lending Platforms

Peer-to-peer (P2P) lending systems have revolutionized the way lenders and borrowers connect by facilitating direct interactions, bypassing traditional financial institutions. Platforms such as Faircent, LenDenClub, i2iFunding, and Lendbox offer access to credit for individuals who may not have a bank account or sufficient collateral or credit history to qualify for conventional loans. These platforms use algorithms to assess creditworthiness, enabling loans for both individuals and small businesses, which in turn fosters entrepreneurship and drives economic growth in underserved areas.

Significant fintech developments, including crowdfunding and P2P lending, have created alternative funding sources that provide crucial financial opportunities for small businesses and individuals who are often overlooked by traditional financial intermediaries (Taherdoost, 2023). Research by Sabilla (2023) explores how P2P lending enhances financial inclusion in fintech. Her findings highlight that P2P lending platforms have made a substantial impact by offering new financing opportunities to small businesses and individuals who are underserved by traditional banks. The study underscores the importance of consumer protection policies and governmental support to ensure the sustainable growth of P2P lending platforms.

Blockchain and Cryptocurrency

Blockchain technology and cryptocurrency have the potential to transform financial services for the unbanked. By eliminating the need for intermediaries, blockchain-based solutions offer a secure and transparent alternative to traditional financial infrastructure. In regions where banking services are limited or non-existent, cryptocurrencies provide individuals with a safe way to store money and conduct transactions. The decentralized and secure transaction mechanisms enabled by blockchain technology, which underpins cryptocurrencies, foster financial inclusion by reducing costs and enhancing trust, particularly in areas with weak or absent financial infrastructure (Arner *et al*., 2018).

Digital Lending Platforms

In India, fintech has played a pivotal role in expanding financial inclusion, particularly through the widespread adoption of mobile banking services. The extensive reach of mobile phones has enabled platforms like Lending Kart, CapFloat, and MobiKwik to provide essential financial services, even in remote areas. Through user-friendly smartphone applications or basic USSD codes, people can now perform a variety of tasks, such as transferring money, paying bills, and accessing microloans. This newfound accessibility has empowered individuals who were once excluded or underserved by traditional financial systems.

In addition, digital lending platforms have become a crucial means of meeting the credit needs of India's underbanked and unbanked populations. Companies such as MobiKwik, CapFloat Financial Service, MoneyTap, Lending Kart Technologies Private Limited, and ScoreMe have revolutionized credit access by utilizing innovative credit scoring models and data analytics to quickly and effectively assess borrower creditworthiness. These platforms are opening doors for entrepreneurship and fostering financial growth in previously underserved areas by simplifying the loan application process and eliminating the need for collateral (Fig. **5**).

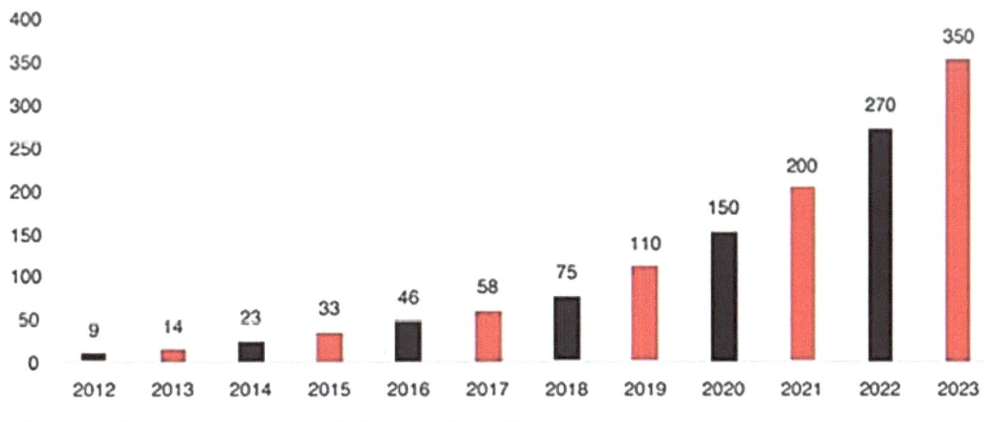

Fig. (5). Growth of digital lending in India (in USD billion).
Source: CIBIL, BCG Google 2018 Digital Lending Survey (2018).

As highlighted in joint research by Omidyar Network and Boston Consulting Group (2019), India's digital lending industry is projected to reach USD 350 billion in 2023, up from USD 110 billion in 2019. As a result, digital lending is expected to become the sector with the largest penetration by digital channels in India, growing from 23% of the country's total loan market in 2018 to 48% by 2023. The COVID-19 pandemic has significantly impacted work practices, accelerating the nationwide push for digitization. However, the devastating second wave of COVID-19 has forced many Indian states to reimpose lockdown-like restrictions, which may present another challenge for the digital lending ecosystem as it recovers from the 2020 lockdowns.

Agent Banking

In 2006, the Reserve Bank of India introduced the 'Business Correspondent Model' as a part of its agent banking initiative. This model allows commercial banks to collaborate with non-bank retail outlets, such as pharmacies, supermarkets, mobile phone stores, microfinance institutions, e-governance centers, and former public servants, to deliver financial services. Despite the promise of agent banking, challenges persist, particularly in India, which has the second-largest unbanked population in the world (Demirguc-Kunt *et al.*, 2018). Over the past decade, the Indian government has rolled out several initiatives to expand the agent network. These include the launch of the Pradhan Mantri Jan Dhan Yojana (PMJDY) in 2014, the Direct Benefit Transfer (DBT) program in 2013, the Aadhaar-enabled Payment System (AePS) in 2010, and the linking of Aadhaar and bank accounts in 2015. Agent banking has gained traction in many developing nations, recognizing its potential to drive financial inclusion (Kochar, 2018). The role of agent banking has been further strengthened by financial innovations, especially in emerging markets.

The comparative Table **3** on financial inclusion indicators for 2023 highlights significant regional disparities in the adoption of digital financial tools and the integration of AI-driven services. Kenya and China lead in both mobile money usage and digital wallet penetration, with Kenya leveraging platforms like M-Pesa and Tala to serve 87% of its adult population, and China demonstrating very high AI-driven credit scoring through Alipay, achieving 89% digital wallet penetration. In contrast, countries like the Philippines and India, while making strides through platforms such as GCash, Tala, and Paytm, still face considerable gaps, with unbanked populations at 35% and 22% respectively. Ghana shows promising growth, with 55% mobile money usage and increasing AI integration via Jumo and Zeepay, although 29% of its adults remain unbanked. The data underscores how AI-powered FinTech solutions significantly influence financial inclusion, yet also reveals the need for tailored strategies to address contextual challenges in underbanked regions.

Table 3. Comparative financial inclusion indicators (2023).

Country	Mobile Money Users (% of Adults)	AI-Driven Credit Scoring Use	Digital Wallet Penetration	% Unbanked Adults	Source
Kenya	87%	High (via M-Pesa, Tala)	73%	17%	FSD Kenya, Tala
India	41%	Moderate (Tala, Paytm)	62%	22%	RBI, World Bank
China	82%	Very High (Alipay)	89%	13%	Ant Group
Ghana	55%	Growing (Jumo, Zeepay)	47%	29%	BoG, CGAP
Philippines	38%	Moderate (GCash, Tala)	51%	35%	BSP, GSMA

Source: Author's own creation.

MANAGERIAL IMPLICATIONS

The rise of Artificial Intelligence (AI) in fintech offers tremendous potential for enhancing the efficiency, personalization, and security of financial services. However, the technology also brings along challenges that need to be carefully managed to maximize its benefits.

Advantages of AI in Fintech

1. **Efficiency and Automation**: One of the major benefits of AI in fintech is automation. By automating tasks like transaction processing, customer queries, and compliance checks, AI enables financial institutions to cut turnaround times significantly. What would normally take hours or days can now be completed in seconds, increasing operational efficiency.
2. **Fraud Detection**: AI's ability to analyze large amounts of real-time data allows it to detect suspicious activities instantaneously. Unlike traditional fraud detection systems, which operate on set rules, AI systems continuously learn from new data, adapting to emerging threats and improving the accuracy of fraud detection. This dynamic approach also helps reduce false positives, thus providing a smoother experience for customers.
3. **Cost Reduction**: AI helps financial institutions reduce operating costs by automating repetitive tasks that would normally require human labor. For example, AI-driven chatbots can handle customer inquiries without the need for human intervention, saving on staffing costs and providing customers with round-the-clock assistance.
4. **Personalization**: By analyzing vast amounts of customer data, AI can offer highly personalized services such as financial advice, product

recommendations, and tailored solutions. The ability to customize experiences not only increases customer satisfaction but also fosters loyalty, which is crucial in a competitive market.

5. **Decision-Making**: AI provides financial professionals with predictive analytics, enabling them to make informed decisions. AI models analyze historical and real-time data to uncover trends and provide predictions that can guide financial institutions in responding quickly to market changes.
6. **Increased Accessibility**: AI helps expand access to financial services for those traditionally excluded from the system, such as individuals without a credit history. By using alternative data sources like transaction behavior and social media activity, AI can create more accurate credit profiles, thus providing underserved populations with access to loans and financial products.

Challenges in AI Adoption

1. **Data Security and Privacy**: With the vast amount of sensitive customer data handled by financial institutions, AI applications present an increased risk of data breaches and misuse. Ensuring robust data security is vital to prevent significant financial, reputational, and regulatory damage. Financial institutions must continuously monitor and strengthen their cybersecurity frameworks.
2. **Regulatory Compliance**: As fintech continues to innovate, regulatory frameworks struggle to keep pace with these advancements. AI systems, especially deep learning models, often operate as "black boxes," making it difficult for financial institutions to explain or justify decisions to regulatory bodies. This lack of transparency can create compliance challenges, particularly when AI is used for sensitive functions like loan approval or credit scoring.
3. **Bias and Fairness**: AI models can unintentionally perpetuate biases, particularly if they are trained on biased data. In financial services, this could lead to discrimination, such as denying loans to certain groups based on historical patterns rather than actual risk. Financial institutions must ensure that their AI models are fair and unbiased by employing diverse data sources and regularly auditing these models.
4. **Integration with Legacy Systems**: Many financial institutions still rely on outdated legacy systems, which may not be compatible with modern AI technologies. Integrating AI solutions with these systems requires significant investments in both time and money, posing a challenge for institutions with limited budgets. Balancing the potential benefits of AI with the costs of system updates can be a tough decision for these institutions.
5. **Talent Shortage**: As AI technology becomes increasingly integral to fintech, there is a growing demand for skilled professionals with expertise in data science, machine learning, and AI. Financial institutions may struggle to recruit and retain the talent needed to develop, implement, and maintain AI systems,

particularly as the demand for these skills rises across industries.

CASE STUDIES

M-Pesa (Kenya): Mobile-Based Financial Inclusion with AI-Driven Credit Scoring

M-Pesa, established by Safaricom in 2007, is one of the most distinguished success stories in mobile money and financial inclusion in Africa. Planned initially to simplify microfinance credit settlements, the platform swiftly progressed into a full-scale mobile money system, permitting users to deposit, withdraw, transfer funds, and pay for goods and services via basic mobile phones. The incorporation of Artificial Intelligence (AI) into M-Pesa's ecosystem came with the development of services like M-Shwari, a partnership between Safaricom and the Commercial Bank of Africa. M-Shwari uses machine learning algorithms to analyze customer behavior—including mobile phone usage, airtime purchases, and transaction histories—to assess credit risk and extend microloans to users without traditional credit histories. AI systems process vast amounts of information to notice behavioral patterns that are linked with solvency, enabling the delivery of custom-made financial products to users. The model circumvents the need for collateral or a formal financial history, which are often barriers for the unbanked population in rural and underserved areas. The macroeconomic impact of M-Pesa has been significant. According to research by Suri and Jack (2016), the platform helped lift approximately 2% of Kenyan households out of extreme poverty, with particularly strong effects among female-headed households. M-Pesa has now expanded to multiple countries, with over 40 million users.

Tala (Global South): Alternative Credit Scoring via AI

Tala is a FinTech company operating in emerging markets such as Kenya, India, the Philippines, and Mexico. It offers instant microloans through a mobile app by utilizing AI-driven alternative credit scoring models. Unlike traditional lenders, Tala does not rely on formal credit histories but instead gathers over 10,000 data points from users' smartphones. These include text messages, app usage, call logs, and bill payment patterns. Machine learning algorithms analyze this metadata to generate a credit profile, allowing Tala to assess the risk level of potential borrowers and determine appropriate loan amounts. The AI system continuously learns and adapts, improving accuracy over time based on repayment behaviors and user interactions. Tala has significantly contributed to increasing financial access, especially for first-time borrowers. Over 85% of its customers had never accessed formal credit before (Suri & Jack, 2016). The company has paid loans to over 6 million clients, demonstrating the success of AI in associating with credit gaps. The real-time, scalable nature of AI-based lending allows Tala to process applications and distribute funds within minutes, making it highly suitable for regions with limited banking infrastructure. By promoting financial inclusion through responsible lending, Tala also contributes to broader economic participation and poverty reduction.

Alipay and Ant Financial (China): AI for Credit, Fraud Detection, and Personalized Finance

Alipay, established by Alibaba Group, is part of the Ant Financial network and is one of the world's most classy FinTech platforms. With over a billion users, it demonstrates how AI can be used at scale to improve financial inclusion and working productivity. AI is embedded throughout Alipay's infrastructure. The Zhima Credit (or Sesame Credit) system utilizes big data and AI to create credit scores based on online shopping behavior, payment history, social connections, and more. This structure permits individuals without old credit records to access financial products, including loans and insurance. AI-driven fraud detection systems also play a vital role. These algorithms identify unusual spending patterns and intervene in real time, enhancing security and trust. Furthermore, robo-advisory services such as Ant Fortune use AI to deliver venture guidance to users, including those with very small revenue, encouraging savings and wealth-building. Alipay's integration of AI has supported China's broader financial inclusion objectives by making digital financial tools reachable even in rural areas. Its success has encouraged regulatory reforms and inspired similar systems globally.

Jumo (Africa): Scalable AI Lending Platform

Jumo is a mobile money services platform working largely in Sub-Saharan Africa and South Asia. It enables mobile network operators and banks to offer digital lending and savings products to underserved populations. Central to Jumo's operations is the use of AI and machine learning to assess credit risk and customised financial services. By analyzing mobile phone usage patterns, transaction records, and behavioral data, Jumo's AI models develop customer profiles and regulate eligibility for monetary products. These real-time credit assessments are particularly valuable in regions where access to formal identification and financial history is limited. Since its beginning, Jumo has disbursed over $3 billion in loans to more than 20 million customers. Its scalable infrastructure and AI-driven decision engines allow for rapid adaptation to various markets and client segments. Jumo also backs financial education by providing users with financial health understandings and nudges to encourage responsible borrowing. This all-inclusive approach improves long-term inclusion and economic empowerment.

CONCLUSION

The present chapter demonstrates that the combination of AI and FinTech signifies a substantial transformation in the financial sector. While AI in fintech offers promising benefits, such as enhanced efficiency, security, and accessibility, it also presents a set of challenges that must be addressed. Financial institutions need to navigate issues related to data security, regulatory compliance, bias, integration with legacy systems, and the talent shortage to fully realize AI's potential. By handling these challenges strategically and ethically, fintech companies can create a safer, more inclusive, and customer-centric financial ecosystem. Properly managed, AI can significantly improve the financial services landscape, driving innovation, inclusivity, and efficiency.

AI is assisting FinTech companies in overcoming significant difficulties, including financial exclusion, regulatory compliance, fraud protection, and consumer engagement, so as to facilitate the development of inclusive, accessible, and secure financial services. In India, the emergence of mobile banking, digital lending, and agent banking illustrates the influence of FinTech on the unbanked and underbanked, demonstrating how technology can revolutionize economies by providing financial opportunities to previously marginalized people. Also, the obstacles, including data security, ethical dilemmas, and interoperability with older systems, persist as significant issues. The pursuit of completely actualizing AI's promise in FinTech necessitates meticulous oversight to guarantee that progress is ethical, equitable, and secure. If FinTech firms continue to utilize AI judiciously, they may establish a robust financial ecosystem that empowers marginalized communities and fosters sustainable economic growth. The FinTech evolution, propelled by AI's capabilities, assures a future in which financial inclusion becomes a reality for billions rather than merely an objective.

REFERENCES

Arner, DW. Buckley, RP. Zetzsche, DA. (2018). *Fintech for Financial Inclusion: A Framework for Digital Financial Transformation.* UNSW Law Research Paper No. 18-87.
[https://ssrn.com/abstract=3245287].

Asian Development Bank, & Wyman, O. (2017). *Accelerating financial inclusion in South-East Asia with digital finance..*
[http://dx.doi.org/10.22617/RPT178622-2]

Brynjolfsson, E., Rock, D., Syverson, C. (2017). *Artificial intelligence and the modern productivity paradox: a clash of expectations and statistics.* Available from: www.nber.org/chapters/c14007.pdf Retrieved: December 24, 2019
[http://dx.doi.org/10.3386/w24001]

Castro, D., New, J. (2016). *The promise of artificial intelligence: 70 Real-World examples.* Available from: www2.datainnovation.org/2016-promise-of-ai.pdf Retrieved: December 27, 2019

Carbó, S., Gardener, E.P.M., Molyneux, P. (2005). Financial Exclusion in the UK. In: Carbó, S., Gardener, E.P.M., Molyneux, P., (Eds.), *Financial Exclusion.* (pp. 14-44). Palgrave Macmillan, UK. [http://dx.doi.org/10.1057/9780230508743_3]

Danladi, S., Prasad, M.S.V., Modibbo, U.M., Ahmadi, S.A., & Ghasemi, P. (2023). Attaining sustainable development goals through financial inclusion: Exploring collaborative approaches to Fintech adoption in developing economies. *Sustainability (Basel), 15*(17), 13039. [http://dx.doi.org/10.3390/su151713039]

Frederick, S. E., Lopez-Acevedo, G. C., Robertson, R., & Vergara Bahena, M. A. (2021). *From jobs to careers: Apparel exports and career paths for women in developing countries.* World Bank Group.. [http://dx.doi.org/10.1596/978-1-4648-1803-5]

GSMA. (2025). *State of the industry report on mobile money 2025: Reaching new peaks.* Available from https://www.gsma.com/sotir/.

Golubev, A., Ryabov, O. (2020). Transformation of traditional financial companies into FinTech. *Proceedings of the International Scientific Conference - Digital Transformation on Manufacturing, Infrastructure and Service,* Association for Computing Machinery. pp. 1-7. [http://dx.doi.org/10.1145/3446434.3446543]

Gomber, P., Kauffman, R.J., Parker, C., Weber, B.W. (2018). On the Fintech Revolution: Interpreting the Forces of Innovation, Disruption, and Transformation in Financial Services. *Journal of Management Information Systems, 35*(1), 220-265. [http://dx.doi.org/10.1080/07421222.2018.1440766]

Goswami, S., Sharma, R.B., Chouhan, V. (2022). Impact of financial technology (Fintech) on financial inclusion (FI) in Rural India. *Universal Journal of Accounting and Finance, 10*(2), 483-497. [http://dx.doi.org/10.13189/ujaf.2022.100213]

Group, I.E. (2015). *Financial Inclusion-A Foothold on the Ladder toward Prosperity? An Evaluation of World Bank Group Support for Financial Inclusion for Low-Income Households and Microenterprises.* World Bank. Available form: https://ieg.worldbankgroup.org/evaluations/financial-inclusion-foothold-ladder-toward-prosperity.

Jennah, H. (2017). *G20/OECD INFE REPORT Ensuring financial education and consumer protection for all in the digital age.* Available from: https://policycommons.net/artifacts/3794239/g20oecd-infe-repot-ensuring-financial-education-and-consumer-protection-for-all-in-the-digital-age/4600067/

Kochar, A. (2018). Branchless banking: Evaluating the doorstep delivery of financial services in rural India. *Journal of Development Economics, 135*, 160-175. [http://dx.doi.org/10.1016/j.jdeveco.2018.07.001]

Leyshon, A., Thrift, N. (1996). Financial Exclusion and the Shifting Boundaries of the Financial System. *Environment and Planning A: Economy and Space, 28*(7), 1150-1156. [http://dx.doi.org/10.1068/a281150]

Lyons, A.C., Scherpf, E. (2004). Moving from unbanked to banked: Evidence from the Money Smart program. *Financial Services Review-Greenwich, 13*(3), 215-232.

Lee, K.F., Qiufan, C. (2018). *AI Superpowers: China, Silicon Valley, and the New World Order.* Houghton Mifflin Harcourt.

Lyons, A., Chang, Y., Scherpf, E. (2006). Translating financial education into behavior change for low-income populations. *Journal of Financial Counseling and Planning, 17*(2), 65-78. Available from: https://papers.ssrn.com/ sol3/papers.cfm?abstract_id=2232122

Lyons, A., Grable, J., Zeng, T. (2017). Infrastructure, urbanization, and the financial inclusion of Chinese households. *SSRN,* 3012453. Available from: https://papers.ssrn.com/sol3/papers.cfm?abstract_id=3012453 [http://dx.doi.org/10.2139/ssrn.3012453]

McCarthy, J., Minsky, M. L., Rochester, N., Shannon, C. E. (2006). A proposal for the Dartmouth summer research project on artificial intelligence. *AI Magazine*, 27(4), 12-14. [http://dx.doi.org/10.1609/aimag.v27i4.1904]

Minsky, M. (1974). *A framework for representing knowledge.* (AI Memo 306). MIT Artificial Intelligence Laboratory..

Organisation for Economic Co-operation and Development. (2015). *National strategies for financial education: OECD/INFE policy handbook.* OECD Publishing..

Rao, A. (2017). A strategist's guide to artificial intelligence. *Strategy+Business.* Available from: www.strategy-business.com/article/A-Strategists-Guide-to- Artificial Intelligence? gko= 0abb5 .

Suri, T., Jack, W. (2016). The long-run poverty and gender impacts of mobile money. *Science, 354*(6317), 1288-1292. [http://dx.doi.org/10.1126/science.aah5309] [PMID: 27940873]

Sabilla, S. (2023). The role of peer-to-peer lending in fintech towards financial inclusion in Indonesia *Jurnal Darma Agung, 31*(2) Available from: https://ejurnal.darmaagung.ac.id/index.php/jurnaluda/article/view/2827

Simon, J.P. (2019). Artificial intelligence: scope, players, markets and geography. *Digital Policy, Regulation and Governance, 21*(3), 208-237. [http://dx.doi.org/10.1108/DPRG-08-2018-0039]

Sahay, M.R., Cihak, M., N'Diaye, M.P., Barajas, M.A., Mitra, M.S., Kyobe, M.A., Mooi, M., Yousefi, M.R. (2015). Financial inclusion: Can it meet multiple macroeconomic goals? *International Monetary Fund.* Available from: https://books.google.com/books?hl=en&lr=&id=tLMaEAAAQBAJ&oi=fnd&pg=PA4&dq=International+Monetary+Fund.+(2015).+Financial+inclusion:+Can+it+meet+multiple+macroeconomic+goals%3F+%5BVideo+file%5D.+Retrieved+from+http://www.imf.org/external/mmedia/view.aspx%3Fvid%3D4543486557001&ots=FgBZLMuynl&sig=fQHMgc0abVEDnCf7RXjk5A9nKGM [http://dx.doi.org/10.5089/9781513585154.006]

Sinclair, S. *Financial exclusion: An introductory survey. Centre for Research in Socially Inclusive Services (CRISIS)*, Heriot-Watt University. Retrieved from https://www.academia.edu/7086629/Financial_Exclusion_An_Introductory_Survey

Taherdoost, H. (2023). Innovations in financial technology and their impact on financial markets. *Journal of Financial Regulation and Compliance, 31*(1), 75-93.

United Nations Secretary-General's Special Advocate for Inclusive Finance for Development (UNSGSA). (2018). *Annual report to the Secretary-General: Financial inclusion – technology, innovation, progress.* https://sdgs.un.org/sites/default/files/publications/2649unsgsa.pdf.

Villasenor, J. D., West, D. M., & Lewis, R. J. (2016). *The 2016 Brookings financial and digital inclusion project report.* Center for Technology Innovation at Brookings. Available from: https://www.fintechfutures.com/files/2016/09/fdip_20160803_project_report.pdf.

CHAPTER 3

Investigating the linkages of HRM Practices and Financial Inclusion: Challenges and Opportunities with reference to Emerging Market Economies (EMEs)

Abhishek Kumar Pandey[1,*], Manish Kumar Singh[2], Nishant Kumar[3] and **Pramod Kumar Upadhyay[4]**

[1] *Department of Management, IILM Academy of Higher Learning, Lucknow, Uttar Pradesh, India*

[2] *Department of Management, School of Management Sciences, Lucknow, Uttar Pradesh, India*

[3] *Deptartment of Management, Faculty of Management Studies, University of Lucknow, Lucknow, Uttar Pradesh, India*

[4] *Department of Commerce, Maharaja Bijli Pasi Government P.G. College, University of Lucknow, Lucknow, Uttar Pradesh, India*

Abstract: The growth and development of an economy largely depend upon its human resources and their contribution to different sectors of the economy. In this case, it is quite interesting to see existing linkages, possible relationships, and key imperatives associated with Human resource management practices with financial inclusion. The present chapter explores and offers a relevant discussion on the interrelated linkages of human resource management practices and their linkages to financial inclusion, with special focus on emerging market economies like India, China, Brazil, and others, which are not only growing faster but setting a distinct image in their efforts of financial inclusion for their citizens and other stakeholders. In this chapter, researchers try to conceptualise the relevant dimensions of HRM with emphasis on financial inclusion in emerging market economies.

Keywords: Emerging market, Economies, Financial, HRM practices, Inclusion.

INTRODUCTION

In the management of organisations and large economic systems, the role of human resources (employees or workforce) cannot be denied. The growth and development of an economy cannot be achieved until its human resources are

* **Corresponding author Abhishek Kumar Pandey:** Department of Management, IILM Academy of Higher Learning, Lucknow, Uttar Pradesh, India; E-mail:abhishekmba0811@gmail.com

Mohammed Majeed, Sofia Devi Shamurailatpam, Parag Sunil Shukla, Ibrahim Osman & Hamidu Gafaru Dokurugu (Eds.)

properly aligned. Its emphasis is on the role of Human Resource Management (HRM), which can boost the productivity, performance, and profitability of any organisation or the core, secondary, and tertiary sectors of the economy as well. Human Resource Development (HRD) is known as a crucial component of HRM, which also emphasises training and development initiatives for employees who can better contribute to financial inclusion programs and initiatives in emerging economies. In a review work by Wilson & Briscoe (2004), it is concluded that education and training investment boost national economic growth. It shows that HRM has existing as well as potential linkages with the economic and financial growth of a country.

Exploring the Meaning And Significance of EMEs

In general, the meaning of ***Emerging markets Economies (EMEs)*** can be taken as a developing nation's economy that's growing into global marketplaces is an emerging market economy. Emerging market economies share several traits with developed markets. Strong economic growth, high per capita income, liquid equities and debt markets, foreign investor accessibility, and reliable regulation are some of the characteristics of developed markets (Team & Scott, 2024). Even, it is a general perception that an emerging economy is closer to the transition and race to achieve the status of a developed economy.

State of Financial Inclusion and its policy framework in EMEs

As of the middle of 2018, the Reserve Bank of India (RBI) observed that more than 35 nations, including China, Brazil, and Indonesia (All are emerging market economies), had implemented a national strategy for financial inclusion. The following are some of the common themes that are present in these countries: (i) adhering to a target-based approach (by focusing on particular industries), (ii) enhancing the necessary infrastructure of payment mechanisms, (iii) establishing a robust regulatory framework, (iv) putting an emphasis on last-mile delivery and financial literacy, (v) utilizing innovation and technology, and (vi) periodically monitoring and evaluating the progress that has been made in the realm of financial inclusion (Committee Reports, 2024).

In India, the Jandhan scheme was launched in 2014. It has been a remarkable scheme that has added many people to mainstream financial inclusion. India is widely recognised for its safe and robust digital payment infrastructure. The data in Fig. (**1**) highlights the insights related to robustness in digital transactions:

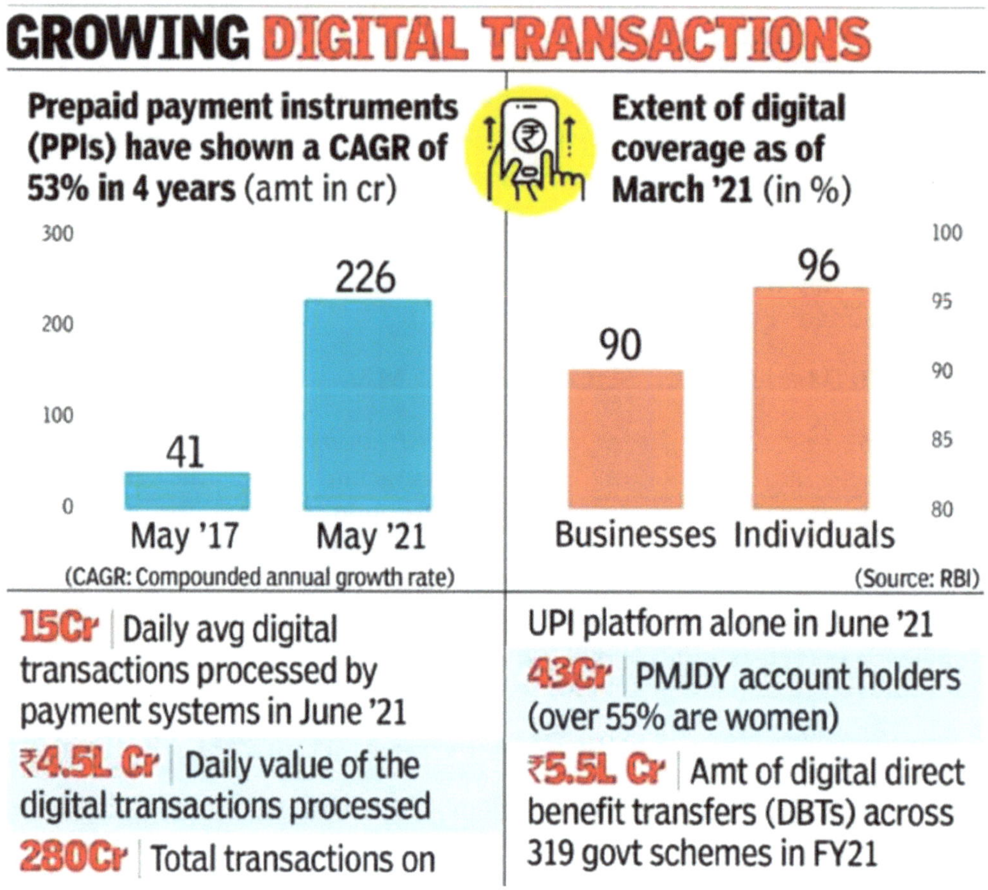

Fig. (1). Growing digital traction.
Source: Times of India (18 August 2021).

A web article states that eighty-four percent of adults in Brazil currently have access to a formal financial account (Findex 2021), which is an increase from seventy percent in 2017 and fifty-six percent in 2011. Brazil has made significant progress in the area of financial inclusion over the past eleven years. Furthermore, Brazil's continued pro-competition attitude to establishing an inclusive digital finance ecosystem and infrastructure, such as the interoperable payments like Pix, has been essential. Additionally, Brazil's evolving open finance laws, which can assist in the flourishing of private sector innovation, have been a significant factor. The ability to contact underprivileged groups has been significantly facilitated by this (*Building Resilience and Financial Health Through Inclusive Finance in Brazil*, 2023).

The quick adoption of digital financial services, such as mobile money and payment applications, by Southern African countries contributed to their overall success in terms of financial inclusion between 2011 and 2021. This fact was disclosed by financial specialists in a webinar. The financial sector in the Southern African region is confronted with several critical issues, including liquidity challenges, debt distress, restricted access to financial services, significant informality, and regulatory constraints (Economic Commission for Africa, 2024).

China has undergone significant development and has gathered extensive experience in inclusive financial systems. As the economy continues to evolve swiftly, along with the reform and transformation of the financial sector, there is an increasing availability of financial services tailored for individuals and enterprises in China, particularly for micro and small enterprises and low-income groups. As reported by the People's Bank of China (PBC) and the China Banking and Insurance Regulatory Commission (CBIRC), by the conclusion of June 2020, the total loans extended to Micro and Small Enterprises (MSEs) and agricultural sectors in China amounted to RMB40.7 trillion and RMB37.8 trillion, representing 24% and 22% of the overall outstanding loans from financial institutions, respectively. As an essential element of financial reform, financial inclusion played a vital role in advancing poverty alleviation and fostering regional economic growth in China (Chen & Yuan, 2021).

The brief insights above offer an overview of how financial reforms and new developments in EMEs promote the holisticness of financial inclusion programs for different stakeholders.

HUMAN RESOURCES MANAGEMENT PRACTICES PROMOTING FINANCIAL INCLUSION

Human Resource Management (HRM) practices can be beneficial in increasing financial inclusion by introducing methods to provide inexpensive financial products and services. Payroll and compensation policies can provide direct deposit and digital payment methods to ensure employees without bank accounts receive their paychecks securely and traceably (Turner *et al.,* 2018). Paying salaries on time prevents employees from taking out predatory loans during financial hardship (Goldberg & Palladini, 2020). Financial literacy training and learning initiatives are also important. HR can improve financial inclusion by teaching employees about budgeting, saving, and investing (Chen & Volpe, 2021). These programs may join with financial institutions to offer financial counselling (Tufano, 2019).HR can enhance financial security by offering emergency money, low-interest loans, and workplace savings programs.

Employees can avoid high-interest loans and develop wealth with these techniques (Hilgert *et al.*, 2021). Health, life, and disability insurance at low prices protects employees in emergencies (Churchill & Matul, 2020). Flexible payroll systems and pay advances, such as on-demand earned wage access, help employees manage short-term financial demands and prevent payday loan use (Smit, 2020).

Advocating for fair salaries and transparent pay structures for low-wage workers reduces income inequality and enhances financial inclusion for at-risk individuals (OECD, 2019). Financial counselling from Employee Assistance Programmes (EAPs) can help employees avoid financial exclusion by managing debt and budgeting finances (Anderson et al., 2018). Diversity, Equity, and Inclusion (DEI) measures in HR, such as hiring from underrepresented populations, enable underprivileged groups who may have had limited access to financial services and economic prospects (Tsang, 2020). Sharia-compliant banking for Muslim employees is an example (Khan, 2019). Pensions and retirement savings accounts support employees, especially those unfamiliar with them, in securing financial futures (Lusardi & Mitchell, 2017).

HR may enhance female financial inclusion by introducing gender-sensitive policies that give women equitable access to financial products and support during maternity leave, improving their financial stability (Folbre & Nelson, 2020). Finally, HR can engage with fintech firms to give digital financial tools like budgeting apps and investment platforms to employees without traditional banking accounts, bridging the digital divide (Philippon, 2019). Training underserved populations on digital finance tools can also help them understand new financial technologies (Beck *et al.,* 2018). These insights clearly indicate that the role of HRM and its practices are quite beneficial in managing and promoting financial inclusion strategies, specifically in emerging market economies.

CONCEPTUALLY LINKING THE HRM PRACTICES WITH FINANCIAL INCLUSION

In the age of technology and various analytics tools, organisations in emerging markets can use the flow diagram below to manage HRM practices and initiatives, and financial inclusion by overcoming the challenges caused by negative outcomes and executing appropriate strategies to enhance the financial inclusion program. The flow diagram in Fig. (**2**) can be considered to link HRM functions and financial inclusion by the organisations:

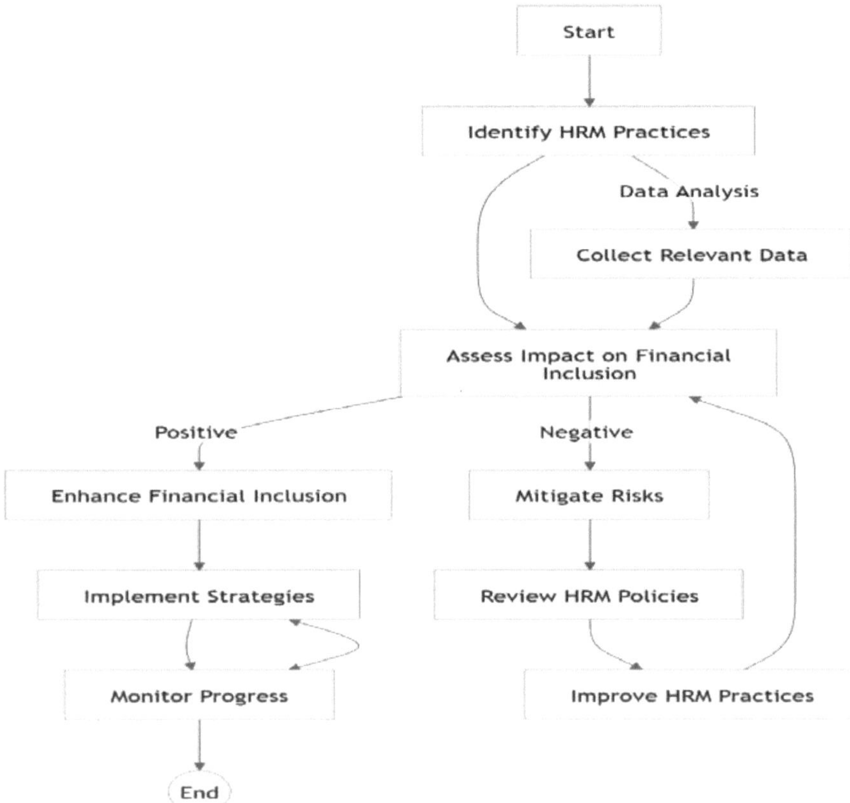

Fig. (2). Flow diagram to understand conceptual linkages of HRM interventions and financial inclusion process.
Source: Researcher's self-created conceptual linkages of HRM and Financial Inclusion with the help of an online tool.

CHALLENGES AND OPPORTUNITIES OF HRM PRACTICES AND THEIR RELATIONSHIP WITH FINANCIAL INCLUSION STRATEGIES AND INITIATIVES

There is limited evidence that HRM practices are connecting with financial inclusion initiatives, but it can be observed that there are many indirect linkages of Human Resources practices that are somehow related to Financial Inclusion and contribute to promoting such initiatives. The practices of Human Resource Management (HRM) play a vital role in influencing the success of organizations, especially when they are integrated with overarching strategies such as financial inclusion. Financial inclusion involves making financial services available to everyone, allowing individuals and businesses to engage fully in the economic landscape (Demirguc-Kunt *et al.,* 2018). Human resource management practices, which cater to recruitment, training, and performance management, are essential in promoting financial inclusion by cultivating an inclusive organizational culture and developing the human capital required to provide accessible financial services. Nonetheless, harmonizing HRM practices with financial inclusion strategies brings forth a mix of challenges and opportunities.

Challenges in Connecting HRM Practices with Financial Inclusion

A significant obstacle in harmonizing HRM with financial inclusion strategies is the presence of skill gaps. Numerous organizations in developing economies encounter challenges in attracting individuals with the required skills and expertise to execute financial inclusion initiatives (Das & Ghosh, 2021). For example, the workforce might not possess the necessary skills in digital financial technologies, which are essential for providing financial services to underserved populations. Another challenge is the reluctance to adapt, as employees may not fully accept new technologies or the transition to more inclusive service delivery models. This may hinder the organization's ability to innovate and respond effectively to the changing needs of financially excluded populations (Bashir & Aslam, 2018). Furthermore, HRM encounters the difficulty of promoting cultural awareness and inclusivity. Financial inclusion frequently focuses on underserved communities, necessitating that employees remain cognizant of and adaptable to various cultural, socioeconomic, and educational contexts. HR professionals must adeptly manage this complexity while ensuring that employees remain engaged and aligned with the overarching objectives of inclusion.

Opportunities for Linking HRM and Financial Inclusion Strategies

On the other hand, there are considerable prospects when HRM practices are effectively integrated with financial inclusion strategies. Through the establishment of strong training and development initiatives, organizations can elevate their workforce's skills, improving their ability to provide inclusive financial services. Beck *et al.* (2020) indicate that investing in training to enhance digital financial literacy can significantly boost the organization's capacity to provide financial services to underserved communities. Moreover, HRM practices that foster diversity and inclusion among employees can improve the organization's capacity to engage with and cater to varied client demographics. A varied team, comprising individuals from different backgrounds, can enhance creativity and deepen the organization's insight into the distinct requirements of diverse communities, thus boosting the success of financial inclusion initiatives (Rao, 2018). Systems that evaluate and enhance employee performance by recognizing their contributions to financial inclusion objectives can also motivate individuals to innovate and embrace inclusive practices.

KEY IMPERATIVES ON HRM & FINANCIAL INCLUSION FOR EMERGING MARKET ECONOMIES AND THEIR RELEVANT STAKEHOLDERS:

The following considerations will be useful if HRM practices can be linked to financial inclusion strategies and initiatives:

a. Employees of the organization need to be trained in the financial inclusion management program. It will be helpful to boost this program in a larger sector of the economic system.
b. Government authorities and policy makers need to be open-minded to formulate conducive policies which can club human resource development (HRD) and its effective utilisation in financial inclusion programs led by different stakeholders like private sector organisations, NGOs, bureaucrats, and private equity investors.
c. There is a need for an updated version of the policy framework that caters to the new age challenges, like the adoption of artificial intelligence, machine learning, and cloud technologies to drive HRM functions, as well as enhancing the inclusive tactics in the financial inclusion program of the country.
d. Emerging market economies need to strengthen such polices that promote Corporate Social Responsibility (CSR) programs, which are also helpful in enhancing the financial inclusion objectives in the economy.
e. National-level employment policies should be framed that specially include the underprivileged sections of society, which will improve the financial inclusion of such people.
f. Emerging Market Economies (EMEs) can promote such a common platform and initiatives, which are helpful in managing issues related to financial inclusion and its relationship with HRM and HRD initiatives.
g. Organisations need to revamp their strategic framework, which must cater to HRM-centric interventions conducive to the financial inclusion program of the related emerging market.
h. EMEs need proper attention to deliver financial inclusion programs and initiatives in a sustainable and quality-centred approach.

EMPIRICAL AND THEORETICAL STRENGTHENING OF HRM-FINANCIAL INCLUSION LINKAGES

While the conceptual framework established in this chapter highlights a strong theoretical connection between Human Resource Management (HRM) practices and financial inclusion, the absence of empirical evidence limits the robustness of the argument. To bridge this gap, data from recent surveys across Emerging Market Economies (EMEs) demonstrate growing adoption of HRM-led financial inclusion initiatives. According to the World Bank Enterprise Surveys (2023), over 42% of formal enterprises in India and 35% in Brazil have integrated digital payroll systems and direct deposit mechanisms, reducing barriers for unbanked employees. Similarly, the ILO's 2022 Human Capital Report revealed that 28% of firms in Kenya and South Africa offer some form of financial literacy training, particularly in the manufacturing and service sectors. These empirical trends validate the conceptual linkages proposed and suggest that HRM strategies are increasingly seen as enablers of inclusive financial ecosystems in EMEs.

To strengthen the academic rigor of this linkage, the argument can be anchored in the Resource-Based View (RBV) of the firm. RBV suggests that sustainable competitive advantage is achieved through the strategic use of valuable, rare, inimitable, and non-substitutable (VRIN) resources. Human capital, developed through robust HRM practices such as employee training, inclusive recruitment, and performance-based incentives, serves as one such strategic asset. Organizations that invest in workforce financial well-being not only improve retention and productivity but also build capabilities that enable them to serve underbanked markets more effectively. Furthermore, Social Exchange Theory offers another lens: it posits that reciprocal relationships between employers and employees—fostered by transparent pay, access to financial tools, and supportive workplace policies—encourage greater trust and engagement. These social bonds can increase participation in formal financial systems, particularly among marginalized groups.

By combining these theoretical perspectives with real-world data, the chapter moves beyond a conceptual narrative to present a more robust, evidence-informed case for integrating HRM into national and organizational financial inclusion agendas. For instance, Nubank in Brazil has reported increased employee satisfaction and digital finance adoption after introducing internal financial education workshops and equity-based compensation. Similarly, Paytm in India has linked employee development programs with outreach to rural communities, demonstrating how HR strategies can create both internal and external financial inclusion impacts.

POLICY RECOMMENDATIONS: THE EIGHT IMPERATIVES

1. Integrate CSR with Financial Inclusion Initiatives: HR departments should embed Corporate Social Responsibility (CSR) into organizational values by incentivizing staff participation in community-based financial literacy campaigns, rural outreach, and support for underbanked populations.

2. Promote AI and Digital HR Solutions for Inclusion and encourage the adoption of AI-driven recruitment and training platforms that reduce geographical, social, and economic biases. AI can help identify underrepresented talent pools and deliver inclusive digital onboarding and micro-learning experiences.
3. Develop Financial Literacy Training for Employees and Communities: HRM must ensure that internal training programs include financial wellness modules—covering savings, mobile banking, and digital wallets—and extend this education to surrounding communities through volunteer HR engagement.
4. Support Inclusive Staffing and Occupation Development Policies: Organizations should adopt equitable hiring practices targeting underserved regions and marginalized groups (e.g., women, rural youth). This includes offering flexible, remote roles and removing traditional credential blockades *via* competency-based assessments.
5. Establish Gender-Inclusive Workplaces and Financial Tools: HR should lead the charge on gender equity by enforcing policies on equal pay, mentorship for women, and workplace harassment protection while also advocating for financial products tailored to women's needs (e.g., maternal savings plans).
6. Forge Public–Private HR Partnerships for Rural Talent Development: Governments and companies should collaborate to build localized talent pipelines—e.g., through vocational training hubs, digital access centers, and job placement platforms targeting financially excluded populations.
7. Design HR Rules that Incentivize Digital Inclusion Champions: Recognize and reward staff who lead digital inclusion projects, such as expanding mobile banking usage, launching community FinTech labs, or advocating open banking frameworks that benefit the unbanked.
8. Monitor and Evaluate Inclusion Metrics within HR KPIs: Embed financial inclusion metrics into HR performance indicators—such as the percentage of recruits from low-income areas or financial access improvements among employees—and report progress annually to key stakeholders.

CONCLUSION

This chapter offers a conceptual understanding of linkages of HRM practices to financial inclusion programs and strategies adopted by organisations operating in emerging market economies. It provides a potential model which can be utilized by the organisations and major EMEs to link HRM practices with Financial Inclusion strategies. The Chapter highlights that although HRM encounters obstacles like skill shortages and reluctance to adapt, the synchronization of HRM practices with financial inclusion strategies presents avenues for enhancing service delivery, fostering innovation, and driving organizational growth. Confronting these challenges with focused recruitment, training, and inclusion strategies can guarantee the effectiveness of financial inclusion efforts. In other words, Emerging Market Economies (EMEs) have the potential to benefit significantly from connecting their human resource management practices with their financial inclusion initiatives. Organizations have the ability to improve their capacity to provide inclusive financial services by placing a higher priority on employee training, cultivating diversity, and revising policy frameworks. This integration has the potential to inspire creativity, inclusivity, and general economic development, which will be to the benefit of areas that are underserved. Corporate sector organisations can refer to this study and get relevant insights and formulate such policies that promote financial inclusion.

REFERENCES

Anderson, R., Berg, A., Brown, K. (2018). Employee assistance programs: Wellness and financial well-being support for employees. *Employee Assistance Research Journal, 35*(2), 45-67.

Bashir, S., Aslam, S. (2018). Employee resistance to change: A case of financial inclusion. *Journal of Organizational Change Management, 31*(1), 45-63.

Beck, T., Demirgüç-Kunt, A., Honohan, P. (2018). Access to financial services: Measurement, impact, and policies. *The World Bank Economic Review, 22*(3), 457-482.

Beck, T., Demirguc-Kunt, A., Levine, R. (2020). Financial inclusion: Measuring progress. *World Bank.*

United Nations Secretary-General's Special Advocate for Inclusive Finance for Development. (2023, June 19). *Building resilience and financial health through inclusive finance in Brazil.* https://www.unsgsa.org/country-visits/building-resilience-and-financial-halth- through-inclusive-finan-e-brazil.

Chen, H., Volpe, R.P. (2021). Financial literacy and education: Theory and research on its role in promoting financial inclusion. *Journal of Consumer Affairs, 55*(1), 85-110.

Chen, W., Yuan, X. (2021). Financial inclusion in China: an overview. *Frontiers of Business Research in China, 15*(1), 4.
[http://dx.doi.org/10.1186/s11782-021-00098-6]

Chakraborty, T., Das, M. B., Singh, R. (2022). *Women's financial inclusion and empowerment in South Asia.* World Bank Publications.

Churchill, C., Matul, M. (2020). *Protecting the poor: A microinsurance compendium.*Geneva: International Labour Office.

Das, A., Ghosh, P. (2021). Skill gap analysis in financial inclusion: Challenges for HRM. *International Journal of Business and Management, 15*(3), 145-158.

Demirguc-Kunt, A., Klapper, L., Singer, D., Ansar, S., Hess, J. (2018). The Global Findex Database 2017: Measuring financial inclusion and the fintech revolution. *World Bank Group.*
[http://dx.doi.org/10.1596/978-1-4648-1259-0]

Diagramming AI - Instantly Design UML & Workflows with AI. (n.d.). Retrieved November 7, 2025, from https://diagrammingai.com/.

Desai, S., Andrist, L. (2010). Gender scripts and age at marriage in India. *Demography, 47*(3), 667-687.
[http://dx.doi.org/10.1353/dem.0.0118] [PMID: 20879683]

Folbre, N., Nelson, J. (2020). For love or money: Care provision and women's work in a changing economy. *Oxford University Press.*

Goldberg, M., Palladini, E. (2020). Managing liquidity in a global financial crisis: The role of on-time salary payments. *International Journal of HR Management, 42*(4), 611-629.

Hasan, Z., Menon, R. (2005). Unequal Citizens: A Study of Muslim Women in India. *Oxford University Press.*

Hilgert, M., Hogarth, J.M., Beverly, S.G. (2021). Household financial management: The connection between knowledge and behavior. *Federal Reserve Bulletin, 89*(7), 309-322.

Jejeebhoy, S.J., Sathar, Z.A. (2001). Women's Autonomy in India and Pakistan: The Influence of Religion and Region. *Population and Development Review, 27*(4), 687-712.
[http://dx.doi.org/10.1111/j.1728-4457.2001.00687.x]

Khan, F. (2019). Islamic banking: A guide to Sharia-compliant finance. *Journal of Islamic Finance, 14*(2), 150-165.

Lusardi, A., Mitchelli, O.S. (2007). Financial literacy and retirement preparedness: Evidence and implications for financial education. *Business Economics, 42*(1), 35-44.
[http://dx.doi.org/10.2145/20070104]

Organisation for Economic Co-operation and Development. (2019). OECD employment outlook 2019: *The future of work.* OECD Publishing..

PRS Legislative Research. (n.d.). *National Strategy for Financial Inclusion (2019–2024).* https://prsindia.org/policy/report-summaries/national-strategy-financial-inclusion

Oxfam India. (2021). *India inequality report 2021: India's unequal healthcare story.* https://www.oxfamindia.org/knowledgehub/workingpaper/inequality-report-2021-indias-unequal-healthcare-story

Philippon, T. (2019). *The FinTech opportunity*, National Bureau of Economic Research Working Paper No. 22476.
[http://dx.doi.org/10.3386/w22476]

Ravindran, T.K.S., Kelkar-Khambete, A. (2008). Women's autonomy and the nutritional status of children in Kerala, India. *Reproductive Health Matters, 16*(31), 165-174.

Rao, P. (2018). The role of diversity in enhancing financial inclusion strategies. *Journal of Human Resources and Financial Management, 12*(2), 23-35.

Smit, D. (2020). On-demand pay: How flexible wage access reduces employee financial stress. *International Journal of Payroll and Benefits Management, 26*(2), 56-64.

Team, I., Scott, G. *Emerging Market Economy: Definition, How It Works, and Examples. Investopedia.*https://www.investopedia.com/terms/e/emergingmarketeconomy.asp#:~:text=Some%20 notable% 20emerging%20market%20economics,a%20higher%20standard%20of%20living (2024, 8 July)

Times of India. (2021, August 18). *Financial inclusion grew 24% across FY17-21: RBI.* https://timesofindia.indiatimes.com/business/india-business/financial-inclusion-gre--24-across-fy17-21-rbi/articleshow/85415519.cms

Tsang, S. (2020). Diversity, equity, and inclusion: Building inclusive financial services for marginalized communities. *Journal of Financial Economics, 15*(2), 221-235.

Tufano, P. (2019). Just finance: Financial inclusion in the digital age. *Harv. Bus. Rev., 97*(2), 132-141.

Turner, M.A., Chen, H., Volpe, R.P. (2018). The role of payroll management in promoting financial inclusion. *Payroll Research Institute Quarterly, 6*(3), 115-132.

Thorat, S., Newman, K.S. (2010). Blocked by Caste: Economic Discrimination in Modern India. *Oxford University Press.*

UN Women. (2021). *Intersectionality resource guide and toolkit: An intersectional approach to leave no one behind.* United Nations Entity for Gender Equality and the Empowerment of Women.
[https://asiapacific.unwomen.org] .

United Nations Economic Commission for Africa. (2024, June 18). *Despite challenges, Southern Africa has improved financial inclusion with adoption of digital financial services.* https://www.uneca.org/stories/despite-challenges%2C-southern-africa-has-improved-finncial-inclusion-with-adoption-of.

Wilson, R. A., & Briscoe, G. (2004). The impact of human capital on economic growth: A review. In P. Descy & M. Tessaring (Eds.), *Impact of education and training: Third report on vocational training research in Europe: Background report* (Cedefop Reference Series No. 54, pp. 13–61). Office for Official Publications of the European Communities. https://wrap.warwick.ac.uk/id/eprint/69101/.

CHAPTER 4

Barriers and Progress in Financial Inclusion for Ever-married Women in India

Naorem Pushparani Chanu[1], **Rabichandra Singh Elangbam**[2,*] and **Virendra Singh**[3]

[1] *School of Liberal Studies and Education, Navrachana University, Vadodara, Gujarat, India*

[2] *School of Business and Law, Navrachana University, Vadodara, Gujarat, India*

[3] *Department of Sociology, Faculty of Arts, The Maharaja Sayajirao University of Baroda, Vadodara, Gujarat, India*

Abstract: This chapter investigates the determinants of account-holding status among ever-married women in India, utilizing data from the National Family Health Survey (NFHS-5) for the period 2019-21. It explores three key aspects of financial inclusion: access to bank or financial institution accounts, mobile phone ownership, and the use of mobile phones for financial transactions. The study examines the relationship between account-holding status and various socio-economic parameters, offering insights into how factors such as place of residence, religion, economic status, education, age, personal occupation, and the husband's education and occupation influence financial inclusion. Methodologically, the analysis combines descriptive statistics and econometric tools to provide a comprehensive understanding of financial accessibility for ever-married women in India. The findings highlight the significant role of these socio-economic factors in shaping women's financial inclusion.

Keywords: Account holding status, Ever-married women, Financial inclusion, NFHS-5.

INTRODUCTION AND BACKGROUND

Financial inclusion plays a critical role in building resilience to economic shocks, particularly for the poorer sections of society. It is a key driver of inclusive development, which developing countries must prioritize to achieve equitable growth. The significance of financial inclusion lies in its ability to empower individuals and communities by providing access to formal financial systems. Currently, around 65 per cent of adults in the poorest developing economies lack

* **Corresponding author Rabichandra Singh Elangbam:** School of Business and Law, Navrachana University, Vadodara, Gujarat, India; E-mails: rabichandrae@nuv.ac.in, rabichandra@gmail.com

Mohammed Majeed, Sofia Devi Shamurailatpam, Parag Sunil Shukla, Ibrahim Osman & Hamidu Gafaru Dokurugu (Eds.)

access to financial services, and only about 20 per cent use formal financial institutions for borrowing and lending (Pazarbasiogl, *et al.*, 2020). Studies have shown that in rural areas of developing countries, many people lack access to formal financing due to barriers such as inconvenience and high transaction costs (Beck & Demirgüç-Kunt, 2008; Karlan *et al.*, 2016; Soumaré *et al.*, 2016). However, recent advancements in mobile technology and network availability have enabled rural populations to access digital financial services through formal institutions, bridging the gap caused by the absence of traditional banking infrastructure (Andrianaivo & Kpodar, 2011; Pazarbasioglu *et al.*, 2020; Chatterjee, 2020; Chatterjee & Anand, 2017).

For women, financial inclusion remains a significant challenge due to various socio-economic barriers. Despite these challenges, studies suggest that when women have access to financial services, they are better able to manage and prioritize their budgets independently (Aker *et al.*, 2016; Field *et al.*, 2016). Women's financial inclusion has been shown to improve household consumption levels, particularly for necessities, more effectively than their male counterparts. This not only benefits individual households but also strengthens communities and societies at large (Islam *et al.*, 2014; Ashraf *et al.*, 2010; ILO, 2020). Moreover, financial inclusion empowers women by giving them greater freedom to make employment choices, decisions about marriage and family planning, and even the ability to leave abusive relationships (Aker *et al.*, 2016; Holloway *et al.*, 2017; Suri and Jack, 2016; Garikipati, 2008; Panda, 2014).

According to a 2015 United Nations report, women are particularly vulnerable to poverty due to the unequal distribution of labor and lack of control over economic resources. The report revealed that one in ten women globally is not consulted about how her own earnings should be spent. Additionally, only 58 per cent of women worldwide have formal financial accounts, compared to 65 per cent of men. This gap is even more pronounced in South Asia (Demirgüç-Kunt *et al.*, 2015).

Despite the critical role of financial inclusion in women's empowerment, there is a paucity of academic literature on this subject, particularly in India. Even more limited are studies focusing on the financial inclusion of ever-married women. In order to bridge this research gap, the present study seeks to fill this gap by analyzing the factors that determine the account-holding status of ever-married women in India, using data from the National Family Health Survey-5 (NFHS-5). Through this analysis, the study aims to provide deeper insights into the economic empowerment of women in India and the role of financial inclusion in fostering this empowerment.

METHODS

The study utilizes data from the NFHS-5 to analyse the account-holding status of ever-married women in India. A binary logistic regression model is employed to predict the determinants of the account-holding status, where the dependent variable has a binary outcome. The NFHS data classifies women into six marital status categories: never married, currently married, married but '*gauna*' not performed, widowed, separated, and deserted. For the binary logistic regression, a dummy variable was created, assigning a value of '0' to women who were never married and '1' to women in any of the other categories—termed "ever-married women" for the purposes of this analysis.

The independent variables include: place of residence (rural or urban); religion (Hindu, Muslim, Christian, and others); total number of children ever born; economic status (poorest, poorer, middle, richer, and richest); highest year of education of the respondent; age (15-49 years); use of mobile phones for financial transactions; social group (Scheduled Caste, Scheduled Tribe, or no caste/no tribe); occupation of the respondent (formal workers, not working, informal workers, agricultural workers, and others); total years of the husband's education; and husband's occupation (formal workers, informal workers, agricultural workers, and others). Empirically, when there is only one predictor variable X_1, the probability of Y is predicated as follows:

$$P(Y) = \frac{1}{1 + e^{-(b_0 + b_1 X_{1i})}}$$

Where P(Y) is the probability of Y occurring, 'e' is the base of natural logarithms, b_0 is a constant, X_1 is a predictor variable .

Similarly, when there are more than one predictor variables, the equation becomes:

$$(Y) = \frac{1}{1 + e^{-(b_0 + b_1 X_{1i} + b_2 X_{2i} + \cdots + b_n X_{ni})}}$$

The resulting values from the logistic regression equation vary between 0 and 1. A value close to 0 indicates that Y is unlikely to have occurred, and a value close to 1 indicates that Y is likely to have occurred.

RESULTS

Descriptive Findings

Accessibility to Bank or Financial Institution Accounts for Ever-married Women in India

In Fig. (**1**), the NFHS-5 shows that 78 per cent of the ever-married women have an account in a bank or in any financial institution, while 22 per cent do not have any of such accessibility. When we break down the data by major selected states in India, Tamil Nadu ranks the highest in terms of account-holding status among ever-married women, followed closely by Karnataka, Odisha, Telangana, Chhattisgarh, and Jharkhand. This trend indicates that women in these states have greater financial inclusion, which could be attributed to state-level efforts promoting banking access, government welfare schemes (Kochar, *et al.*, 2022), and financial literacy programs targeted specifically at women (Banerjee, *et al.*, 2021). However, a surprising observation is that the percentage of ever-married women without a bank account or access to any financial institution is higher in Gujarat compared to states like Bihar, Odisha, and Rajasthan, which are generally considered to be less economically well-off. This raises an interesting question, given Gujarat's reputation as one of India's more economically developed states, with higher industrialization, a robust business environment, and relatively better infrastructure.

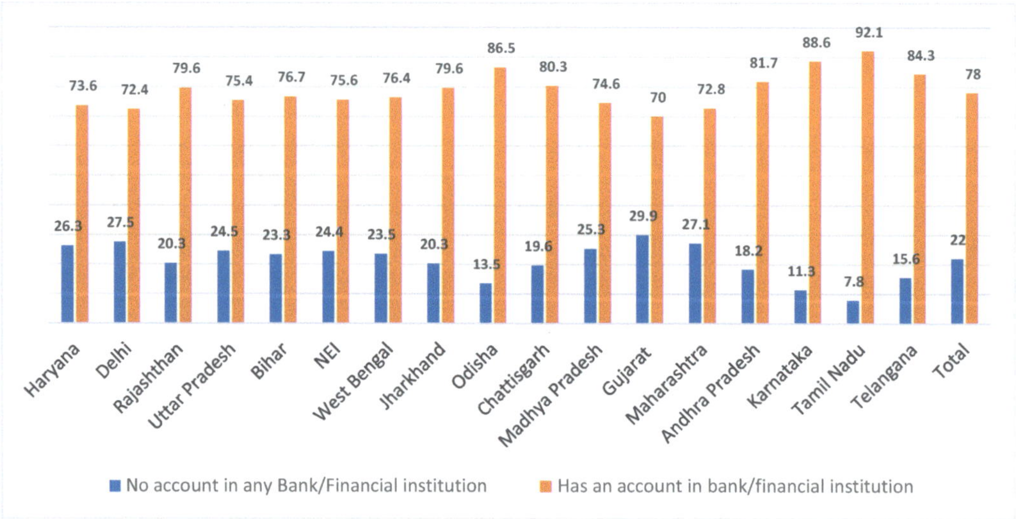

Fig. (1). Account holding status of ever-married women in select states of India.
Source: NFHS-5

Several factors could explain this anomaly in Gujarat. This may be attributed to factors such as cultural and social norms (Ghosh and Vinod, 2017; Pavitra, 2024), which may still limit women's financial independence, despite the state's economic progress. In more conservative regions of Gujarat, women may rely on male family members for financial matters, resulting in lower account ownership. It may be important to note that Gujarat has a large informal economy (Economic survey, 2021-22), especially in sectors like textiles, handicrafts, and agriculture, where many women work but lack formal employment contracts or bank accounts. Informal workers often face difficulties accessing financial services due to the absence of required documentation or a steady income. Another possibility may be that women in Gujarat may rely on alternative financial systems such as community savings groups or informal credit systems, which may be perceived as more accessible or trustworthy compared to formal banks or other financial institutions. (Deininger and Liu, 2013; Sedai, *et al.*, 2021)

However, states like Tamil Nadu, Odisha, and Karnataka may have effectively implemented schemes like the Tamil Nadu Women's Development Corporation, SHG (Self-Help Group) bank linkage programs, and microfinance initiatives that might have contributed to the higher account ownership in these regions (Banerjee, *et al.*, 2015; Kochar, *et al.*, 2022).

The NFHS-5 data categorized economic status into five groups in Table **1**: poorest, poorer, middle, richer, and richest. It was found that the percentage of account holders among ever-married women from the middle class, richer, and richest sections of society was higher compared to those in the poorest and poorer categories. A closer examination of account-holding status based on economic status across different major states of the country revealed varying trends.

Table 1. Percentage distribution of account-holding status of ever-married women based on their economic status across major states of India.

Major State	Poorest	Poorer	Middle	Richer	Richest
Haryana	0.8	7.2	14.9	27.4	49.4
Delhi	0.3	1.7	5.4	19.2	73.2
Rajasthan	10.6	19.9	22.3	23.8	23.2
Uttar Pradesh	20.5	25	19.1	16.6	18.5
Bihar	38	27.6	17.4	10.6	6.1
NEI	21.8	30.2	23.4	16.9	7.5
West Bengal	29.7	26.1	18.4	15.6	10
Jharkhand	40.3	23.9	16.2	10.4	9
Odisha	31.8	25.9	20.8	14	7.4

(Table 1) cont.....

Major State	Poorest	Poorer	Middle	Richer	Richest
Chhattisgarh	25.7	24.3	20.8	16.2	12.7
Madhya Pradesh	28.5	22.6	17	15.2	16.5
Gujarat	6.5	14.2	20.1	27.8	31.2
Maharashtra	6.7	14.5	20.7	27.5	30.4
Andhra Pradesh	3.4	17.5	31.1	31.3	16.4
Karnataka	5.4	16.5	30.6	28.6	18.6
Tamil Nadu	3	13.1	29	29.9	24.8
Telangana	3.6	16.4	27.3	29.7	22.8
All India Total	16.5	20.3	20.7	20.9	21.3

Source: NFHS-5

In states such as Haryana, Delhi, Gujarat, Maharashtra, and Karnataka, the proportion of ever-married women with bank accounts was significantly higher among the richer and richest sections of society. This suggests that women from economically better-off sections have greater access to financial services compared to women from disadvantaged sections in these states. (Banerjee, *et al.*, 2021)

On the other hand, in states like Uttar Pradesh, Bihar, Northeast India (NEI), West Bengal, Jharkhand, Odisha, Chhattisgarh, and Madhya Pradesh, the highest percentage of ever-married women with bank accounts was found among the poorest and poorer sections. These states are generally less urbanized, have weaker infrastructure, and face stronger social barriers, which may constrain financial inclusion. However, government initiatives such as the Jan Dhan Yojana have likely enabled women from poorer sections to open accounts, contributing to this trend.

However, in states like Andhra Pradesh, Karnataka, Tamil Nadu, and Telangana, account ownership was highest among middle-class ever-married women, indicating a different economic dynamic. The findings suggest the need for further research to fully understand the factors influencing these variations across states.

Use of Mobile Phone for Financial Transactions

Our analysis shows that 59 per cent of ever-married women in India own a personal mobile phone, while nearly 46 per cent still do not. Although the proportion of ever-married women owning mobile phones is relatively high, only 23 per cent of them use their phones for financial transactions. This means that around 77 per cent of married women in India, despite owning a mobile phone, do not utilize it for financial transactions. According to a report by Women's World Banking (2022), a majority of women in India are self-employed in the informal sector, where most transactions are still carried out using cash rather than digital financial platforms. This reliance on cash-heavy transactions diminishes the importance of using mobile phones for financial purposes.

When we further analyze this scenario in terms of major states in India, Karnataka, Haryana, Delhi, and Maharashtra perform comparatively better in terms of mobile phone usage for financial transactions. However, in states such as Bihar, West Bengal, Gujarat, Odisha, and Chhattisgarh, the gap between women who own a mobile phone but do not use it for financial transactions is significantly higher compared to other major states.

Further analysis in Fig. (**2**) of mobile phone usage among ever-married women for financial transactions reveals that it is typically women from the richer or richest segments of the population who use mobile phones for financial purposes. However, this trend does not hold consistently across all major states in India. For example, in Bihar and Northeast India (NEI), the distribution of ever-married women using mobile phones for financial transactions is more spread across the poorest, poorer, and middle-class segments (Garg, 2021; Kulkarani and Ghosh, 2021). Interestingly, Table **2** shows that, in Bihar, women from the richer and richest sections of society use their mobile phones for financial transactions far less than those in the economically disadvantaged groups. This could be due to specific state policies and schemes influencing the data (Arora, 2020), but further research is needed to fully understand the underlying causes.

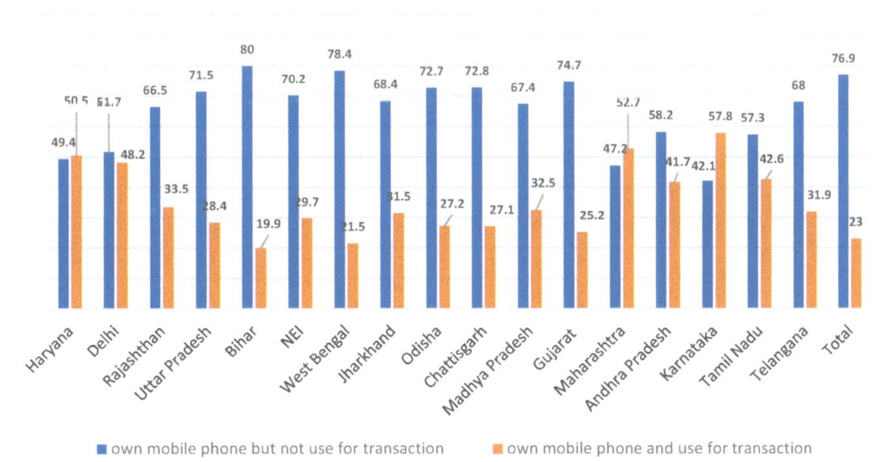

Fig. (2). Percentage of ever-married women using a mobile phone for financial transactions.
Source: NFHS-5.

Table 2. Percentage distribution of ever-married women using mobile phones for financial transactions across major states of India.

Select States	Poorest	Poorer	Middle	Richer	Richest
Haryana	0.25	1.31	6.13	12.65	79.67
Delhi	0	0	3.16	10.94	85.9
Rajasthan	2.07	6.1	11.46	25.21	55.16
Uttar Pradesh	8.45	16.69	16.06	20.73	38.06
Bihar	23.36	24.92	22.65	14.78	14.28
NEI	11.4	21.72	23.71	29.54	13.64
West Bengal	10.6	9.87	6.47	23.17	49.89
Jharkhand	15.8	15.7	15.24	16.73	36.53
Odisha	8.07	12.01	18.76	31.47	29.69
Chhattisgarh	9.33	13.85	18.92	21.22	36.68
Madhya Pradesh	9.82	12.45	10.76	19.08	47.88
Gujarat	1.6	3.54	9.47	23.51	61.88
Maharashtra	1.44	4.42	15.43	16.66	62.06
Andhra Pradesh	2.95	2.21	15.93	37.57	41.35
Karnataka	2.2	7.35	23.06	30.52	36.87
Tamil Nadu	0.48	4.43	19.06	30.17	45.86
Telangana	1.44	6.68	8.82	32.17	50.88
Total	13.5	19.2	21.5	23.1	22.5

Source: NFHS-5.

In NEI, the women using mobile phones for financial transactions primarily belong to the richer class, followed by the middle and poorer sections. It appears that the ever-married women from either the poorest or the richest classes in this region are the ones least likely to use their mobile phones for financial purposes. In the case of ever-married women belonging to the richest category, it might be that men in the household are responsible for managing finances, with women often not engaged in work (Kochar, *et al.*, 2022). On the other hand, in the poorest households, men may be the primary earners, while women assist with domestic duties, limiting their participation in financial matters (Banerjee *et al.*, 2021)

Cultural Norms and Intersectionality in Women's Empowerment

Ever-married women in India face a complex set of socio-cultural and structural barriers shaped by deeply entrenched patriarchal norms. Traditional gender roles rooted in cultural beliefs often assign women subordinate positions in decision-making, particularly in financial matters (Desai & Andrist, 2010). In many households, husbands or elder male family members dominate economic decisions, limiting women's autonomy and access to financial resources (Chakraborty *et al.*, 2022). These dynamics reinforce dependence and curtail empowerment, especially in rural and semi-urban areas. The practice of dowry and son preference continues to shape the socio-economic value of women, often affecting their access to education, nutrition, and healthcare. According to Jejeebhoy and Sathar (2001), these cultural norms are not only embedded in family structures but also perpetuated by community expectations and informal social sanctions. Intersectionality adds a critical layer to understanding these barriers. Caste, religion, and regional disparities compound the experiences of discrimination and inequality faced by ever-married women. Dalit and Adivasi women, for instance, often suffer from dual marginalization—both gender-based and caste-based exclusion (Thorat & Newman, 2010). Muslim women also face specific disadvantages due to socio-religious conservatism and limited access to public spaces and employment (Hasan & Menon, 2005).

Recent empirical studies suggest that these intersecting identities significantly influence women's mobility, access to education, employment, and exposure to mass media—factors known to contribute to women's empowerment (Ravindran & Kelkar-Khambete, 2008). A report by UN Women (2021) highlights that despite improvements in literacy and labor force participation among women in some regions, progress remains uneven across caste and religious groups, underscoring the need for intersectional policy responses. Moreover, the COVID-19 pandemic exacerbated existing disparities. Dalit and Muslim women, who often work in informal sectors, faced higher job losses and food insecurity, revealing the fragility of empowerment gains in the face of systemic inequality (Oxfam India, 2021).

Cultural Norms and Male-Dominated Financial Decision-making

In many Indian households, entrenched patriarchal norms continue to relegate women to subordinate roles, particularly in financial decision-making. Even when women contribute economically, their autonomy in financial matters is often curtailed by prevailing beliefs that men possess superior financial acumen. This dynamic is especially pronounced in rural areas, where traditional gender roles are more rigidly enforced. Studies indicate that women frequently consult male family members—husbands, fathers, or brothers—before making significant financial decisions, reflecting deep-seated cultural perceptions of male financial authority. Moreover, the persistence of dowry practices, despite legal prohibitions, underscores the commodification of women within marital arrangements. Dowry-related pressures not only perpetuate financial dependence but also expose women to domestic violence and, in extreme cases, femicide. The societal expectation for women to "adjust" and endure marital hardships further entrenches their economic and social vulnerability.

Intersectionality Caste, Religion, and Socio-economic Status

The concept of intersectionality is pivotal in understanding the multifaceted barriers faced by ever-married women in India (Haq, 2013). Caste and religion intersect with gender to create unique challenges that vary across different social strata (Dey & Orton, 2016).

1. **Caste Dynamics:** Dalit and Adivasi women often encounter compounded discrimination due to their caste status. Their narratives reveal systemic marginalization, where caste-based hierarchies within patriarchal structures exacerbate their oppression (Dey & Orton, 2016). These women frequently face barriers in accessing education, employment, and healthcare, limiting their avenues for empowerment.
2. **Religious Influences:** Religious doctrines and community practices can further restrict women's autonomy. In some communities, religious norms dictate women's roles and behaviors, often limiting their participation in public life and decision-making processes (Dey & Orton, 2016). These restrictions can hinder women's access to financial resources and opportunities for empowerment.
3. **Socio-economic Factors:** Women residing in urban slums or impoverished rural areas face additional hurdles due to limited access to education and economic opportunities (Dey & Orton, 2016). Studies focusing on urban slums in Chennai highlight how caste and class intersect to restrict married women's access to resources, thereby impeding their socio-economic empowerment.

Furthermore, disparities in labor force participation among women from different caste backgrounds underscore the complex interplay of social factors. While women from lower castes may have higher participation rates due to economic necessity, they often remain confined to informal sectors with limited prospects for advancement. Addressing the barriers to empowerment for ever-married women in India necessitates a nuanced understanding of the cultural and intersectional factors at play (Haq, 2013). Policies aimed at enhancing women's autonomy must consider the deep-rooted male-controlled norms that influence financial decision-making within families. Concurrently, interferences must be subtle to the intersecting characteristics of caste (class), religion (faith), and socio-economic status that uniquely affect women's experiences. Empowerment approaches should be personalized to rip to shreds these encrusted structures of domination, fostering a situation where all women can work out their activities and make a reasonable contribution to the world.

Econometric Analysis

Summary Statistics

Table **3** presents the descriptive statistics on the account-holding status of ever-married women based on various socio-economic factors in India. According to NFHS-5 data, 78 per cent of ever-married women aged 15-49 years have an account in a bank or any financial institution, while 22 per cent do not have access to such facilities. Interestingly, a significant majority of these women with access to financial institutions are from rural areas, whereas the percentage is notably lower in urban areas. Regarding religious affiliation, the majority of account holders are Hindus, with most of them falling within the 25-29 age cohort.

Table 3. Summary of descriptive variables.

Characteristics	Percentage of Women with a Bank Account	Percentage of ever-married Women with a Bank Account
Place of Residence	-	-
Urban	31.8	30.6
Rural	68.1	69.3
Religion	-	-
Hindu	75.6	76.9
Muslim	12.6	12.1
Christians	6.5	6
Others	5.1	4.8
Total children ever born	1.7 (0.16) [mean]	2.3(0. 16) [mean]
Economic status	-	-
Poorest	16.5	17.5
Poorer	20.3	20.6
Middle	20.7	20.6
Richer	20.9	20.2
Richest	21.3	20.8
Highest Years of Education of the respondent	4.2 (0,8) [mean]	4.1(0, 8) [mean]
Age	-	-
15-19 years	14	2
20-24 years	16	11.7
25-29 years	16.9	18.9
30-34 years	15	18.7

(Table 1) cont.....

Characteristics	Percentage of Women with a Bank Account	Percentage of ever-married Women with a Bank Account
35-39 years	14.3	18.3
40-44 years	11.6	14.9
45-49 years	11.9	15.3
Use of a mobile phone for financial transactions	-	-
own a mobile phone but do not use it for financial transactions	82.2	82.6
Own and use a mobile phone for financial transactions	17.7	17.3
Social group	-	-
SC	83	83.4
ST	12	11.6
No caste no tribe*	4.9	4.9
Religion	-	-
Hindu	75.6	76.9
Muslim	12.6	12.1
Christian	6.5	6
Others**	5.1	4.8
Occupation of the respondent	-	-
Formal workers@	66.7	64
Not working	6.6	6.3
Informal work$	10.5	11.3
Agriculture	14.3	16.5
Others	1.7	1.8
Total years of husband's education	-	8.1 (0, 20) [mean]
Husbands occupation	-	-
Formal workers	Na	22.4
Informal work	Na	39.7
Agricultural work	Na	32.2
Others	Na	5.6

Source: NFHS-5.

*No caste/no tribe comprises those who belong to the 'General' category and 'OBCs'

*'Others' comprises religions other than Hindu, Muslim, and Christian

*Formal workers comprise those who are professionals/technicians/managerial/clerical/sales

*Informal workers comprise those who provide services in household/domestic work/skilled/unskilled manual work

Binary Logistic Regression Model: Determinants of Account Holding Status of Married Women in India

The binary logistic regression analysis reveals several key findings regarding the financial inclusion of ever-married women in India. It is found that ever-married women residing in urban areas are less likely to have an account in a bank or any financial institution compared to those living in rural areas. This indicates that rural women may benefit more from financial inclusion initiatives, possibly due to targeted government schemes aimed at rural populations (Deininger & Liu, 2013; Banerjee *et al.*, 2015; Bhatia & Singh, 2019; Kochar *et al.*, 2021). In terms of religion, Muslim and Christian married women are less likely to have bank accounts compared to their Hindu counterparts, suggesting lower financial accessibility among minority religious groups. This could be because of religious beliefs and practices of a minority group, especially among the poorer sections of society (Narayana & Shaghishna, 2021). Interestingly, the analysis shows no significant relationship between the total number of children ever born and the likelihood of having a bank account. This implies that financial inclusion is not influenced by family size, but rather by other socio-economic factors. Furthermore, when considering economic status and age, the results indicate that ever-married women across all economic sections and age groups are equally likely to have access to financial services.

Again, ever-married women who own mobile phones and use them for financial transactions are significantly more likely to have financial accessibility than those who own phones but do not use them for such purposes. This highlights the growing role of digital financial tools in enhancing women's financial inclusion. Social group analysis shows that those ever-married women from the General and OBC categories are more likely to have financial access compared to those from the Scheduled Castes (SCs).

Regarding occupation, the study finds that ever-married women who are not employed, those involved in informal work, or engaged in agricultural work are less likely to have financial access compared to those working in the formal sector. Additionally, the education level of the husband plays a crucial role; as the husband's education increases, so does the likelihood of the wife having financial accessibility. For instance, our analysis shows that if the husband is engaged in agricultural or informal economic activities, the wife is less likely to have access to financial services compared to those whose husbands work in formal economic sectors. These findings emphasize the intersection of gender, education, occupation, and social factors in determining financial inclusion among married women (Table **4**).

Table 4. Determinants of account holding status of ever-married women in India.

Variable	Coef.	Std.	z	95%	Interval
Place of Residence *Ref. Rural*	-	-	-	-	-
Urban	-0.1712922***	0.0328825	-5.21	-0.2357407	-0.1068437
Religion *Ref. Hindu*	-	-	-	-	-
Muslim	-0.1880315***	0.0426022	-4.41	-0.2715304	-0.1045326
Christian	-0.4717507***	0.055058	-8.57	-0.5796624	-0.363839
others	-0.0307364	0.0625008	-0.49	-0.1532357	0.0917629
Total children ever born	-0.0406649	0.0501608	-0.81	-0.1389782	0.0576484
Economic status *Ref. Poorest*	-	-	-	-	-
poorer	0.2404479***	0.0491209	4.9	0.1441726	0.3367232
middle	0.3569025***	0.0492648	7.24	0.2603453	0.4534597
richer	0.3204113***	0.0502361	6.38	0.2219504	0.4188722
richest	0.3257047***	0.0541174	6.02	0.2196366	0.4317728
Highest year of education	0.0414098***	0.0079016	5.24	0.025923	0.0568966
Age *Ref. 15-19 years*	-	-	-	-	-
20-24 years	0.333997***	0.0437417	7.64	0.2482648	0.4197291
25-29 years	0.5346217***	0.0484352	11.04	0.4396905	0.6295529
30-34years	0.7088682***	0.0560361	12.65	0.5990394	0.818697
35-39years	0.8034451***	0.0616498	13.03	0.6826138	0.9242765
40-44years	0.8011293***	0.0688729	11.63	0.6661409	0.9361177
45-49years	0.9013284***	0.0740982	12.16	0.7560986	1.046558
Use of mobile for financial transactions *Ref. own mobile phone but do not use it for financial transactions*	-	-	-	-	-
Own and use a mobile phone for financial transactions	1.086254***	0.0423326	25.66	1.003284	1.169225
Social group *Ref. SC*	-	-	-	-	-
ST	0.1185144	0.0502989	2.36	0.0199304	0.2170984
no caste no tribe	0.1349822**	0.0648647	2.08	0.0078498	0.2621146
-	-	-	-	-	-

Variable	Coef.	Std.	z	95%	Interval
Occupation of the respondent *Ref. Formal workers*	-	-	-	-	-
Not working	-0.9260597***	0.0983957	-9.41	-1.118912	-0.7332077
Informal work	-0.5317858***	0.0888428	-5.99	-0.7059146	-0.357657
Agriculture	-0.782778***	0.0874196	-8.95	-0.9541173	-0.6114388
Others	-0.5191948	0.1400967	-3.71	-0.7937793	-0.2446103
Total years of husband's education	0.0101212**	0.0030257	3.35	0.0041908	0.0160515
Husbands occupation *Ref. Formal workers*	-	-	-	-	-
Informal work	-0.0610811	0.0421102	-1.45	-0.1436156	0.0214533
Agricultural work	-0.124675*	0.0493344	-2.53	-0.2213686	-0.0279814
Others	-0.1971208**	0.0696442	-2.83	-0.3336209	-0.0606206
Constant	1.440061	0.1547896	9.3	1.136679	1.743443

n=65956; LRchi2(27)=231.36; Prob>chi2=0.0000; Log Likelihood=-1321.83; Pseudo R2=0.0805.
Level of significance ***p<0.01, **pp<0.05, *p<0.1.

CONCLUSION

Financial inclusion for women across all strata of society is crucial, as it not only helps remove barriers to inclusive growth but also fosters positive changes in household consumption, decision-making related to employment, and the mitigation of issues like abusive marriages. In many developing countries, closing the gender gap in financial inclusion remains a significant challenge. Nevertheless, various initiatives have been undertaken to address these disparities, with some notable successes. This study focuses on the determinants of financial inclusion for ever-married women in India, utilizing secondary data from the NFHS-5. The findings reveal that, on average, approximately 78 per cent of ever-married women across all states possess financial accounts. In only a few states, such as Maharashtra and Karnataka, do more women utilize mobile phones for financial transactions.

In terms of economic status categorized by income, ever-married women from the richest sections of society are more likely to engage in financial transactions than those from poorer sections in most states. However, exceptions exist in states like Bihar and Northeast India, where the majority of financial transactions come from women in lower to middle-income groups. Additionally, women in rural areas tend to have higher rates of bank account ownership compared to their urban counterparts, likely due to the implementation of financial inclusion programs like the Pradhan Mantri Jan Dhan Yojana.

The study also explores other socio-economic determinants that influence whether a woman holds a bank account. Ever-married women from rural areas are more likely to have financial accounts than those from urban areas. In terms of religion, Hindu women are more likely to have bank accounts compared to women from other religious backgrounds. Middle-income women are more likely to have accounts than women from other income levels, and older women are also more likely to have financial accessibility. Additionally, while owning a mobile phone increases the likelihood of having a bank account, merely owning a mobile phone without using it for financial transactions does not. In terms of social categories, women from the General category (no caste, no tribe) have a higher likelihood of holding a bank account.

Employment plays a significant role as well, with women working in the formal sectors being more likely to have bank accounts compared to those in informal or agricultural work. The husband's education level and type of employment also correlate with the woman's likelihood of financial inclusion—wives of men with more years of education and those employed in the formal sector are more likely to have bank accounts. The study concludes that the account-holding status of ever-married women is influenced by multiple factors, including place of residence, religion, economic status, education, age, personal occupation, and the education and occupation of their husbands.

REFERENCES

Arora, R.U. (2020). Digital Financial Services to Women: Access and Constraints. *Gender Bias and Digital Financial Services in South Asia.,* Leeds: Emerald Publishing Limited.51-72.
[http://dx.doi.org/10.1108/978-1-83867-855-520201004]

Banerjee, A.N., Hasan, I., Kumar, K., Philip, D. (2021). The power of a financially literate woman in intra-household financial decision-making. *Available at SSRN,* 3246314.

Banerjee, A., Duflo, E., Goldberg, N., Karlan, D., Osei, R., Parienté, W., Shapiro, J., Thuysbaert, B., Udry, C. (2015). A multifaceted program causes lasting progress for the very poor: Evidence from six countries. *Science, 348*(6236), 1260799.
[http://dx.doi.org/10.1126/science.1260799] [PMID: 25977558]

Beck, T., Demirgüç-Kunt, A. (2008). Access to finance: An unfinished agenda. *The World Bank Economic Review, 22*(3), 383-396.
[http://dx.doi.org/10.1093/wber/lhn021]

Bhatia, S., Singh, S. (2019). Empowering women through financial inclusion: a study of urban slum. *Vikalpa, 44*(4), 182-197.
[http://dx.doi.org/10.1177/0256090919897809]

Chatterjee, A. (2020). Financial inclusion, information and communication technology diffusion, and economic growth: a panel data analysis. *Information Technology for Development, 26*(3), 607-635.

[http://dx.doi.org/10.1080/02681102.2020.1734770]

Chatterjee, A., Anand, N. (2017). *Financial inclusion, information and communication technology diffusion and economic growth: A panel data analysis.* MSE Working Paper 165. Chennai: Madras School of Economics. Available from: https://www.mse.ac

Deininger, K., Liu, Y. (2013). Economic and social impacts of an innovative self-help group model in India. *World Development, 43*, 149-163.
[http://dx.doi.org/10.1016/j.worlddev.2012.09.019]

Dey, A., & Orton, B. (2016). Gender and caste intersectionality in India: An analysis of the Nirbhaya case 16 December 2012. In M. L. Anderson, H. D. Danowitz, & A. L. Thomas (Eds.), *Gender and race matter: Global perspectives on being a woman* (Advances in Gender Research, Vol. 21, pp. 87–105). Emerald Group Publishing..
[http://dx.doi.org/10.1108/S1529-212620160000021006]

Garg, C. (2021). Is Mobile Phone Use Invading Multiple Boundaries? A Study of Rural Illiterate Women in India. *Indian Journal of Gender Studies, 28*(1), 29-45.
[http://dx.doi.org/10.1177/0971521520974845]

Ghosh, S., Vinod, D. (2017). What constrains financial inclusion for women? Evidence from Indian micro data. *World Development, 92*, 60-81.
[http://dx.doi.org/10.1016/j.worlddev.2016.11.011]

Haq, R. (2013). Intersectionality of gender and other forms of identity. *Gender in Management: An International Journal, 28*(3), 171-184.
[http://dx.doi.org/10.1108/GM-01-2013-0010]

Karlan, D., Kendall, J., Mann, R., Pande, R., Suri, T., Zinman, J. (2016). Research and impacts of digital financial services. *NBER Working Paper 22633.*Cambridge: National Bureau of Economic Research. Available from: http://www.nber.org/papers/w22633
[http://dx.doi.org/10.3386/w22633]

Kochar, A., Nagabhushana, C., Sarkar, R., Shah, R., Singh, G. (2022). Financial access and women's role in household decisions: Empirical evidence from India's National Rural Livelihoods project. *Journal of Development Economics, 155*, 102821.
[http://dx.doi.org/10.1016/j.jdeveco.2022.102821] [PMID: 35241869]

Kulkarni, L., Ghosh, A. (2021). Gender disparity in the digitalization of financial services: challenges and promises for women's financial inclusion in India. *Gender, Technology and Development, 25*(2), 233-250.
[http://dx.doi.org/10.1080/09718524.2021.1911022]

Pavitra, R. (2024) Digital Financial Transaction Practices among Urban and Rural Women. *Digital Skill Development for Industry 4.0.,* Auerbach Publications.259-270.
[http://dx.doi.org/10.1201/9781003504894-21]

Pazarbasioglu, C., Mora, A.G., Uttamchandani, M., Natarajan, H., Feyen, E., Saal, M. (2020). Digital Financial Services. *World Bank Group.* Available from: https://www.worldbank.org

Sedai, A.K., Vasudevan, R., Alves Pena, A. (2021). Friends and benefits? Endogenous rotating savings and credit associations as alternative for women's empowerment in India. *World Development, 145*, 105515.
[http://dx.doi.org/10.1016/j.worlddev.2021.105515]

Soumaré, I., Tchana Tchana, F., Kengne, T.M. (2016). Analysis of the determinants of financial inclusion in Central and West Africa. *Transnational Corporations Review, 8*(4), 231-249.
[http://dx.doi.org/10.1080/19186444.2016.1265763]

Women's World Banking. (2024). *Enabling digital payments for women in India.* https://www.womensworldbanking.org.

CHAPTER 5

From Innovation to Impact: The New Era of Sustainable Finance

Nidhi Upendra Argade[1,*] and **Manisha Pawar**[1]

[1] *Department of Accounting and Financial Management, Faculty of Commerce, The Maharaja Sayajirao University of Baroda, Vadodara, Gujarat, India*

Abstract: This chapter examines how regulatory laws, investor demand for ethical investments, and corporate accountability drive sustainable finance's transformation. It highlights how innovation, through financial instruments like green bonds and digital platforms, is shaping the future of sustainable finance and influencing industries and economies worldwide. The chapter also examines how sustainable finance affects economic development, social well-being, and environmental sustainability, as well as regulatory inconsistencies and market volatility. It identifies opportunities for further integration of sustainable finance and examines how emerging technologies like artificial intelligence and blockchain are expected to drive future trends, creating a more sustainable global financial system.

Keywords: Digital finance, Fintech, Financial instruments, Innovation, Sustainable finance.

INTRODUCTION

The current focus on shareholder wealth maximization and short-term results has led to externalizing social and environmental costs, producing sustainable outcomes. Markets often fail to account for the long-term value of these impacts. To address future challenges, a paradigm shift is needed, proposing a sustainable value creation framework that fully considers the costs of environmental and social (Fatemi & Fooladi, 2013). Sustainable Finance (SF) is a developing domain that incorporates Environmental, Social, and Governance (ESG) considerations into financial decision-making (Edmans & Kacperczyk, 2022). It seeks to direct funds towards projects and activities that provide a beneficial societal effect while guaranteeing sustained financial returns. The integration of ESG issues has compelled financial institutions, investors, and governments to embrace SF as a

* **Corresponding author Nidhi Upendra Argade:** Department of Accounting and Financial Management, Faculty of Commerce, The Maharaja Sayajirao University of Baroda, Vadodara, Gujarat, India; E-mail:nidhiu.argade-afm@msubaroda.ac.in

Mohammed Majeed, Sofia Devi Shamurailatpam, Parag Sunil Shukla, Ibrahim Osman & Hamidu Gafaru Dokurugu (Eds.)

remedy for global crises, including climate change, resource depletion, and social inequality (Ionescu, 2021).

Financial markets, which formerly prioritised profits, increasingly value sustainability for long-term development and stability. This transformation relies on innovation to create new financial instruments, business models, and technologies that solve sustainability issues and boost economic development. However, the path to SF is not without its challenges. Lack of standardised frameworks and indicators for ESG performance makes it difficult for stakeholders to measure the genuine effect of their investments. Integrating sustainability into mainstream financial products demands major changes in risk assessment, regulatory compliance, and stakeholder involvement. Smaller companies without the means to invest in sustainability may find this difficult. Despite these challenges, SF offers vast opportunities. The growing demand for green bonds, social impact investing, and ESG-focused funds reflects a broader recognition that sustainability can be a driver of long-term financial performance. Furthermore, advancements in fintech, such as AI and blockchain, offer tools to enhance transparency, efficiency, and traceability in SF practices. Due to governmental pressure, technological advances, and changing customer expectations, SF may change. As global awareness of climate change and social inequality continues to rise, financial institutions will be expected to play a more proactive role in addressing these issues. SF, therefore, will not only be a trend but a necessity, influencing how businesses operate, investments are made, and long-term value is created.

This chapter explores the various innovations that are driving SF and how they are making a tangible impact on the global cconomy. Thc study also examines the opportunities and challenges that lie ahead in this dynamic field.

LITERATURE REVIEW

SF has gained momentum globally as a response to increasing environmental and social challenges. Several studies have identified key drivers that push the agenda of SF. Ziolo *et al.* (2020) have examined that the World Bank and International Monetary Fund emphasize the need for increased development finance to achieve the 17 Sustainable Development Goals (SDGs). The connection between SF and the SDGs among OECD countries in the European Union (EU), excluding SDG 6 and SDG 14, is limited due to data limitations. The findings indicate that a more SF model correlates with better progress towards various SDGs, particularly in social, environmental, and economic sustainability. Edmans and Kacperczyk (2022) studied how SF has become a core focus for companies and investors, integrating ESG issues into key financial decisions. Its rise is driven by financial relevance, nonfinancial contributions, and evolving investor preferences, as explored in the Special Issue articles.

Innovation is a major force shaping the evolution of SF. Technologies such as blockchain, AI, and big data are enhancing transparency, reducing transaction costs, and enabling the traceability of sustainable investments. Musleh Al-Sartawi *et al.* (2022) explored SD, ESG investment, and how AI might help creditors, investors, and company managers make long-term financial choices. AI's sustainability difficulties and prospects are highlighted. This editorial also sheds light on AI applications and models in sustainable investing, going beyond problem-solving. A rigorous examination of SF and blockchain integration has been limited despite their popularity. Ren *et al.* (2023) employed a comprehensive bibliometric approach to explore how blockchain impacts SF, revealing its widespread application across various industries, its long-term influence on smart cities and the sharing economy, and its potential for integration with other technologies to enhance SF development.

SF has shaped worldwide economies and businesses. The study by Alshehhi *et al.* (2018), which examined the impact of corporate sustainability on financial performance, reached a conclusion similar to the earlier review by Friede *et al.* (2015): there is growing interest but a lack of consensus among researchersWhile 78% of the 132 papers report a positive relationship, research methods and a focus on corporate social responsibility (CSR) over sustainability concepts hinder conclusions, and limited studies from developing countries suggest further research.

RESEARCH GAP

Since the drivers, innovations, and impacts of science fiction have been extensively examined in the existing literature, there are still numerous voids. There is a scarcity of research that has investigated the potential of SF to be implemented in emerging nations, as the majority of studies have concentrated on established markets and significant institutional investors. Additionally, there is a dearth of exhaustive studies that evaluate the long-term economic advantages and hazards of incorporating sustainability into financial strategies. Furthermore, although the significance of technology in the advancement of science fiction is acknowledged, additional research is required to comprehend the practical implications and obstacles associated with the integration of emergent technologies, including Artificial Intelligence (AI), blockchain, and big data, into the financial sector. Finally, there is an opportunity to investigate the potential for global regulatory frameworks to be harmonised in order to facilitate the extensive implementation of SF strategies across various sectors and regions.

This research endeavours to address these deficiencies by examining the challenges and opportunities for science fiction in both developed and developing markets, as well as the primary drivers and innovations. The role of emergent technologies in influencing the future of this field is a particular focus.

Rationale of the Study

The urgent need for SD highlights the importance of understanding SF in both developed and developing economies. Existing research has largely focused on large institutional investors and developed markets, leaving significant gaps regarding effective implementation in emerging economies. This study aims to investigate these gaps by analysing the long-term economic benefits and risks of integrating sustainability into financial strategies. Additionally, it will explore the implications of emerging technologies such as AI, blockchain, and big data for SF. Harmonizing global regulatory frameworks is another crucial aspect that can support the adoption of SF strategies. By examining key drivers and innovations, this research will provide valuable insights to facilitate sustainable investment practices. Ultimately, the study aspires to contribute to a more comprehensive understanding of SF's role in shaping global economies and industries.

OBJECTIVES OF THE CHAPTER

1. To comprehend the primary factors that influence sustainable finance globally.
2. To examine the influence of innovation on the future of sustainable finance worldwide.
3. To investigate the influence of sustainable finance on global economies and industries.
4. To ascertain both the challenges and possibilities associated with the implementation of sustainable finance strategies worldwide.
5. To anticipate future developments and the changing role of technology in sustainable finance.

KEY DRIVERS OF SUSTAINABLE FINANCE

SF is not merely a trend but a fundamental shift in how finance is approached. This transition has been driven by several key factors that underscore the need for sustainability in financial markets. Below, we explore these drivers in detail, providing an understanding of their significance and impact on the evolving landscape of finance.

Climate Change and Environmental Awareness

As climate change causes increasing sea levels, natural catastrophes, biodiversity loss, and unusual weather patterns, the financial sector is being called upon to handle environmental risks (Ionescu, 2021). Economic stability is significantly endangered by climate-related hazards. Over the past few decades, there has been a substantial increase in the financial losses associated with extreme weather events, including wildfires, hurricanes, and flooding (Battiston *et al.*, 2021).

The financing of climate solutions is significantly influenced by financial institutions. Banks, asset managers, and institutional investors can achieve substantial environmental benefits by switching investments from fossil fuels to renewable energy and by providing funding for projects that are designed to mitigate climate change. Green bonds, for example, have emerged as a popular financial instrument designed specifically to fund climate and environmental projects. Guyana, India, Indonesia, Maldives, Ethiopia, Bangladesh, China, Ecuador, Philippines, Brazil, Thailand, and Rwanda have either established or are in the process of establishing a national climate change fund. (Hogarth, 2012). Investors are becoming more cognisant of the tangible hazards associated with climate change, including disruptions to supply chains and property damage. They also recognize transition risks, where policy changes or shifts towards a low-carbon economy could impact the financial performance of carbon-intensive industries. Consequently, an increasing number of investors are incorporating climate risk assessments into their investment strategies, with a focus on companies that exhibit resilience to climate-related risks and adhere to sustainable practices.

The Paris Agreement, established in 2015, aimed to restrict global warming to below 2°C and to strive for a limit of 1.5°C. To meet these targets, trillions of dollars in investments are required in green technologies, infrastructure, and energy (Global Landscape of Climate Finance 2019, 2019). This international framework has pushed countries to set more ambitious climate goals, encouraging private and public investors to align their financial strategies with global climate objectives.

Corporate Social Responsibility (CSR) and Stakeholder Pressure

CSR denotes a company's dedication to operating in an ethical and sustainable manner. While the concept of CSR has existed for decades, it has gained new importance in recent years as consumers, employees, and investors increasingly demand accountability from companies. Growing Stakeholder Pressure: Companies are facing growing pressure from their stakeholders-customers, employees, shareholders, and communities—to adopt more balanced and socially responsible practices (Hou, 2019). Consumers are more informed and vocal about environmental and social issues, preferring to engage with brands that align with their values. Similarly, employees are more inclined to work for organizations that prioritize sustainability and ethical practices.

Companies that integrate CSR into their business models tend to perform better in the long run (Van de Velde *et al.*, 2005). Studies have shown that firms with robust CSR strategies have lower risks, higher employee engagement, and stronger brand loyalty. Moreover, investors are increasingly looking for companies with strong CSR credentials as part of their ESG (Environmental, Social, and Governance) considerations. In response to stakeholder pressure, companies are focusing on sustainability not just as a public relations exercise but as a key element of their long-term strategies. They are issuing sustainability reports, improving supply chain transparency, and committing to reducing their carbon footprints. SF facilitates this shift by providing the necessary capital for businesses to fund these initiatives. For instance, sustainability-linked loans offer companies financial incentives (such as lower interest rates) to meet specific environmental or social performance targets. Companies that fail to consider their social and environmental responsibilities may face reputational damage, which can lead to financial losses and a decline in market value.

Government Policies and Global Regulatory Frameworks

Government policies and regulatory frameworks are crucial in promoting SF. Regulations that mandate corporate transparency, environmental disclosures, and sustainability practices have created a more favourable environment for sustainable investment. Many governments have introduced policies that incentivize or require businesses to operate sustainably. Governments around the world have established carbon markets, which allow companies to trade carbon credits as a way of reducing their emissions. The EU's Emission Trading System (EU ETS), for example, sets a cap on the total amount of greenhouse gases that companies in certain sectors can emit (Christiansen & Wettestad, 2003). Organizations that lower their emissions within the established limit may sell their surplus credits to other entities. This generates a financial incentive for enterprises to decrease their carbon footprint. Through the issuance of sovereign green bonds, governments are also significant participants in SF. These bonds are used to finance environmentally favourable projects, including renewable energy infrastructure, reforestation programs, and climate adaptation initiatives. The risk of private investments in sustainable initiatives is mitigated by government funding, which renders them more appealing to investors. The majority of financial institutions in Indonesia adhere to SF laws. However, without real regulatory control, durable results are hard to achieve (Setyowati, 2023). Beyond national policies, global initiatives like the United Nations SDGs(SDGs) have established a universal framework for sustainability (Saxena *et al.*, 2021). The risk of private investments in sustainable initiatives is mitigated by government funding, which renders them more appealing to investors. The majority of financial institutions in Indonesia adhere to SF laws.

Technological Advancements and Digital Finance

Technological innovation has been a catalyst for change in SF, enabling new models of financing and investment that were previously impossible or impractical. The rise of fintech, blockchain, and big data analytics has revolutionized the way investors access and analyse sustainable financial products (Hussain *et al.*, 2023). Financial technology (fintech) has democratized access to SF by providing new platforms for retail investors to engage with ESG-friendly investments. Fintech apps allow individuals to track the environmental and social impact of their investments in real time, offering tools that assess the carbon footprint of portfolios and suggest ways to improve sustainability performance. Crowdfunding platforms have also emerged, allowing investors to directly fund green projects and social enterprises. Blockchain technology, with its decentralized and immutable ledger system, provides a transparent and tamper-proof way to track the flow of capital in SF. For instance, blockchain can be used to ensure the traceability of green bonds, verifying that funds are being used as promised. It can also track the carbon credits traded in emission markets, providing confidence to investors that environmental targets are being met. Big data analytics enables investors to assess the sustainability of their portfolios by analysing vast amounts of ESG data from multiple sources. Machine learning algorithms can sift through this data to identify companies with strong ESG performance, predict financial risks related to climate change, and recommend investment strategies that align with sustainability goals. Investors can now make more informed decisions based on real-time ESG data, leading to better outcomes for both financial returns and sustainability objectives.

South Korea, China, and Japan are promoting green innovation and finance to balance Asian economic development with environmental sustainability. Increase multifactor productivity, green patent registrations, and green bond issuances. Their ability to drive green foreign direct investment and ESG disclosures will influence the shift toward sustainable growth models (Tolliver *et al.*, 2021).

The Shift in Investor Preferences Towards ESG Investments

Perhaps the most transformative driver of SF is the growing demand from investors for ESG investments. ESG factors are becoming an integral part of investment strategies, with a growing number of institutional and retail investors seeking to align their portfolios with their values (Lopez-de-Silanes *et al.*, 2024). Investors are recognising that organisations that implement robust ESG policies are more likely to outperform their competitors over the long term. ESG considerations contribute to improved financial performance by mitigating risks, improving operational efficiency, and enhancing reputation. For example, companies that focus on energy efficiency can reduce operational costs, while those with strong governance practices are less likely to face scandals or regulatory fines. ESG funds, green bonds, and sustainability-linked loans are now commonplace in the portfolios of asset managers, pension funds, and insurance companies.

The key drivers of SF reflect a broader shift in the global economy towards more responsible and ethical financial practices. Climate change, corporate responsibility, regulatory frameworks, technological advancements, and evolving investor preferences are all converging to reshape the financial landscape, paving the way for a more sustainable future.

INNOVATIVE FINANCIAL INSTRUMENTS FOR SUSTAINABILITY

SF has become increasingly central in addressing the environmental and social challenges faced by our global economy. One of the key ways through which this transformation is taking place is *via* the development of innovative financial instruments that aim to allocate capital in ways that promote sustainability. These instruments include green bonds, social impact bonds, carbon markets, sustainable investment funds, and blended finance initiatives, all of which encourage investments that generate both financial returns and positive societal or environmental outcomes. Below is a detailed exploration of these innovative financial instruments for sustainability.

Green Bonds and Sustainability Bonds

Green Bonds are debt securities issued to raise capital for projects that have positive environmental benefits. The funds raised from these bonds are earmarked for projects such as renewable energy installations, clean transportation, sustainable agriculture, and energy-efficient buildings (Maltais & Nykvist, 2020). It has become one of the most popular instruments for financing environmentally friendly projects, particularly among governments, financial institutions, and corporations that are looking to align their financial approaches with sustainability goals. Governments and corporations can raise funds through green bonds to help finance large-scale projects aimed at reducing carbon emissions, protecting biodiversity, or increasing energy efficiency. This lets investors support environmental goals while making money. The London-based non-profit Climate

Bonds Initiative has tracked the green-branded market since 2009. It publishes an annual report on the global green bond market (Banga, 2019).

Sustainability Bonds: While green bonds are exclusively focused on environmental projects, sustainability bonds are a broader category of debt instruments used to fund both social and environmental initiatives. These bonds support projects that address a wide range of sustainability issues, such as affordable housing, access to healthcare, and renewable energy development (Mocanu *et al.*, 2021).

Social Impact Bonds

Social Impact Bonds (SIBs) are a financial mechanism that links the payment of returns to the accomplishment of specific social outcomes. Unlike traditional bonds, SIBs are not a form of debt but rather a performance-based contract between public sector bodies, private investors, and service providers (Fraser *et al.*, 2018). Investors in SIBs provide direct capital to fund social programs, and the government or another outcome funder repays the investors only if the program meets its predefined objectives. Social Impact Bonds fund social services aimed at addressing issues such as education, healthcare, homelessness, and criminal justice reform. For instance, a government may issue an SIB to reduce recidivism rates among former prisoners. If the outcomes are not met, the investors may lose some or all their capital, thereby transferring the financial risk away from the public sector. SIBs offer several advantages. They encourage innovation in social services by funding programs that may not have access to traditional forms of financing. Additionally, because repayment is contingent on results, they ensure that public funds are spent efficiently. Despite these challenges, SIBs represent an important step towards using financial markets to address social issues. Social Impact Bonds (SIBs) in the EU serve as innovative financial instruments that link investors, social service providers, and public administrations to achieve measurable social outcomes while ensuring financial sustainability. Despite their potential to support public welfare systems, SIBs face challenges related to economic complexities and legal frameworks, necessitating further socio-economic research for effective implementation (Pasi, 2014).

Carbon Markets and Emission Trading Systems

Carbon markets are financial systems designed to diminish greenhouse gas (GHG) emissions by allowing companies to purchase and trade carbon credits. Two primary forms of carbon markets exist: voluntary carbon markets and compliance-based markets, which operate under government regulations. Renewable energy helps lower carbon emissions in the short term, aiding U.S. carbon neutrality, with increases in renewable energy having a more pronounced effect than decreases. SF contributes to emissions reduction over a longer period, with a direct but slower impact compared to renewable energy, while its indirect effect on emissions through renewable energy takes time but is notably significant (Qin *et al.*, 2022).

Emission Trading Systems (ETS): The most prominent example of a compliance-based carbon market is the Emission Trading System (ETS), often referred to as "cap-and-trade" systems. In an ETS, governments set a cap on the total amount of emissions allowed in a particular industry or economy. Companies that exceed their emission limits must buy carbon credits from companies that have reduced their emissions and have surplus credits to sell (Narassimhan *et al.*, 2018). Over time, the cap is gradually reduced, ensuring that overall emissions decrease. Voluntary carbon markets are particularly popular among companies seeking to enhance their corporate sustainability programs and demonstrate leadership in climate action. However, carbon markets have also faced criticism for issues such as carbon leakage (where emissions are simply shifted to regions without regulations) and the risk of greenwashing. Strengthening governance and ensuring the credibility of carbon offset projects are key to maximizing the potential of these markets.

Sustainable Investment Funds and ETFs

Sustainable Investment Funds: These are investment vehicles that allocate capital based on ESG criteria. Sustainable investment funds aim to create returns while encouraging positive social or environmental outcomes (Mervelskemper *et al.*, 2014). They invest in enterprises that are leaders in ESG performance, such as firms with strong environmental policies, ethical labour practices, and transparent governance structures.

Exchange-Traded Funds (ETFs): Sustainable ETFs are another innovative instrument that provides investors with varied coverage to companies with strong ESG profiles. ETFs are funds that trade on stock exchanges like individual stocks, allowing investors to buy shares of a basket of ESG-focused companies (Su, 2018). The popularity of sustainable ETFs has surged in recent years, as they offer a low-cost and liquid way to invest in sustainability. Investors can choose from a wide range of ESG-focused ETFs, such as those that target clean energy companies or firms with gender-diverse leadership teams.

Blended Finance: Public and Private Sector Partnerships

Blended finance is an innovative approach to mobilizing private sector capital for SD by combining it with public or philanthropic funding (Ostojić *et al.*, 2024). The goal of blended finance is to leverage public or concessional funds to de-risk investments in high-impact projects that may not be attractive to private investors due to perceived risks. This approach is particularly useful in sectors such as infrastructure, renewable energy, and climate resilience, where large amounts of capital are needed, and risks can be high. In a typical blended finance structure, public or philanthropic capital is used to absorb certain risks, such as political or currency risk, making the project more attractive to private investors. This can take the form of guarantees, first-loss capital, or grants. By reducing the overall risk profile, blended finance encourages private sector participation in projects that contribute to SD. It has become a critical tool for financing SD in emerging markets and developing countries. These regions often face significant challenges in attracting private investment due to high perceived risks. Blended finance helps to unlock capital for projects that can deliver significant social, environmental, and economic benefits, such as building clean energy infrastructure or improving access to healthcare.

Examples of Blended Finance Initiatives: Blended finance structures have been used in a wide range of sectors, from renewable energy projects to healthcare initiatives. For example, the Global Environment Facility (GEF) has used blended finance to support projects that reduce biodiversity loss and combat climate change. Similarly, the SD Investment Partnership (SDIP) works to facilitate blended finance deals that support the SDGs by bridging the gap between public and private sector investments.

Innovative financial products include green bonds, social impact bonds, carbon markets, sustainable investment funds, and blended finance, which help transition to a sustainable global economy. Investors may profit while improving society by investing in projects and businesses that emphasize environmental and social aims. As sustainability demands rise, these financial innovations will shape finance's future.

THE ROLE OF TECHNOLOGY IN SUSTAINABLE FINANCE

The financial sector is undergoing a technological revolution, and the incorporation of sustainability initiatives is reshaping the allocation of capital toward investments that are socially and environmentally conscious. Financial institutions can achieve unprecedented sustainability by utilizing cutting-edge technologies such as fintech, blockchain, Artificial Intelligence (AI), big data, and digital platforms. Below is a detailed exploration of how technology is reshaping SF.

Fintech's Contribution to SF

Financial technology (Fintech) has emerged as a disruptive force in the finance sector, providing innovative solutions to enhance the efficiency, accessibility, and transparency of financial services (Gomber *et al.*, 2018). Fintech platforms are enabling the creation of new financial products specifically designed for sustainability, such as green investment portfolios, micro-investment platforms, and crowdfunding for environmental projects. Robots can enhance productivity and efficiency in industries by automating tasks, leading to significant advancements in sectors like manufacturing and healthcare. Japan is a leading country in robotics innovation, utilizing robots across various sectors to address labor shortages and improve technological integration. (Macchiavello & Siri, 2022).

Many fintech companies are also driving the adoption of green loans by offering tailored lending solutions for renewable energy projects, energy-efficient building retrofits, and clean technology startups. By simplifying loan application processes and leveraging AI for risk assessment, fintech firms can offer faster and more accessible financing for sustainable projects. In the BRICS nations, environmental sustainability is facilitated by green finance and fintech, whereas economic growth and natural resource rent have a detrimental effect on environmental quality. The BRICS countries should concentrate on the development of green loans and the expansion of the capacity of financial institutions to provide green credit facilities in order to achieve carbon neutrality (Udeagha & Ngepah, 2023).

Blockchain for Transparent and Traceable Sustainable Investments

Blockchain technology, known for its decentralized and immutable ledger, is playing a crucial role in increasing transparency and traceability in SF. Blockchain's inherent properties make it ideal for ensuring that capital intended for sustainability projects is used for its designated purpose, and that all transactions are visible to stakeholders (Calandra *et al.*, 2023).

An organization issues green bonds or sustainability bonds, and blockchain can track the flow of funds to ensure they are being allocated to approved green projects. This transparency reduces the risk of greenwashing, where organizations falsely claim environmental benefits, and increases investor confidence (Dorfleitner & Braun, 2019). In carbon markets, blockchain has the potential to enhance the trading of carbon credits by preventing double-counting of credits and ensuring accurate tracking of emissions reductions. By digitizing carbon credits on a blockchain, organizations can easily buy, sell, and retire credits in a secure and transparent manner.

AI-Driven Sustainability Solutions in Finance

Artificial Intelligence (AI) is transforming the financial industry by providing advanced tools to analyze vast amounts of data, predict trends, and automate processes. In the context of SF, AI offers significant advantages in identifying sustainability risks, optimizing investment strategies, and enhancing reporting on ESG metrics (Sadati *et al.*, 2024). AI-driven models can assess environmental risks, such as the potential impact of climate change on financial portfolios, by analyzing data from diverse sources, including satellite imagery, climate models, and social media. Financial institutions can use these insights to develop strategies that mitigate the risks associated with environmental degradation or extreme weather events. AI-powered platforms can identify investment opportunities that align with ESG principles by analyzing financial data alongside sustainability metrics. For example, AI algorithms can process non-financial data, such as a company's carbon footprint or social impact initiatives, to recommend stocks, bonds, or other assets that meet both financial and sustainability criteria. This helps investors optimize their portfolios while supporting sustainability goals.

Big Data and Analytics for ESG Reporting and Assessment

Big Data and analytics are indispensable instruments for evaluating and disclosing the sustainability performance of financial instruments and organizations. With the help of big data, financial institutions can access real-time information and provide more accurate assessments of their sustainability efforts (Belinky *et al.*, 2022). Big data enables the continuous monitoring of ESG performance across diverse metrics, such as energy consumption, waste management, employee diversity, and board independence. This allows companies to generate detailed ESG reports that meet the demands of regulators, investors, and stakeholders.

The Rise of Digital Green Banks

Digital Green Banks are a new class of financial institutions that operate exclusively online and focus on financing environmentally sustainable projects. By leveraging digital technology, green banks are able to streamline operations, reduce costs, and allocate capital more efficiently toward green projects (Alonso, 2023). These banks use digital tools to automate the lending process, assess borrower eligibility, and offer customized green loans with lower interest rates or incentives for achieving sustainability goals. Technology plays a pivotal role in advancing SF by improving access, transparency, and efficiency. From fintech innovations that democratize green investments to blockchain's ability to ensure transparent and traceable transactions, and AI's capacity for optimizing sustainability solutions, these technological tools are reshaping the financial landscape.

IMPACT OF SF ON GLOBAL ECONOMIES

SF, a sector in the financial sector that is expanding at a rapid pace, is instrumental in guiding the global economy toward a more inclusive and sustainable future. It involves the incorporation of environmental, social, and governance (ESG) factors into financial decisions, thereby guaranteeing that investments result in favourable social and environmental outcomes. (Ziolo *et al.*, 2017). The impact of SF on global economies is multifaceted, affecting everything from economic growth and employment to industry transitions and the development of emerging economies.

Economic Growth through Green Investments

One of the most direct impacts of SF on global economies is through the channel of green investments, which are investments specifically aimed at projects that have positive environmental outcomes. Renewable energy, energy efficiency, waste management, and sustainable agriculture are among the sectors that are typically the focus of green investments. (Dima *et al.*, 2023). As the demand for sustainable products and services grows, green investments are catalyzing economic growth across the world. The positive influence of green investments, economic openness, and governance efficiency on green economic growth, though technological efficiency and innovation vary among countries. The research suggests that future studies should explore the nonlinear effects of green investment and the role of mediating factors like corruption and governance in influencing green economic growth (Kwilinski *et al.*, 2023).

Creating Employment Opportunities in Green Sectors

Another profound impact of SF is its role in generating employment opportunities, particularly in green sectors. As investments flow into renewable energy, energy efficiency, and other sustainable industries, job creation follows (Aceleanu, 2015). According to the International Labour Organization (ILO), the global economy could generate 24 million new jobs by 2030 as a result of the transition to a sustainable economy (24 million jobs to open up in the green economy, 2018). Among these positions are environmental engineers and sustainability consultants, as well as wind turbine technicians and solar panel installers.

The renewable energy sector has been a particularly significant contributor to the creation of green jobs. For instance, the solar and wind energy sectors have generated millions of employment opportunities on a global scale. Solar photovoltaic (PV) energy alone accounted for 3.8 million positions, while the renewable energy sector employed more than 11.5 million individuals globally in

2020 (Renewable Energy Jobs continue growth to 11 million worldwide, 2020). As countries accelerate their renewable energy adoption, this number is expected to rise significantly.

Additionally, SF facilitates the development of new industries, such as the circular economy, which emphasizes recycling, reuse, and the minimization of waste. These industries not only create employment opportunities but also promote innovation and sustainable business practices, contributing to long-term economic stability and growth.

Transitioning Industries: From Fossil Fuels to Renewables

The acceleration of the transition of industries from fossil fuels to renewable energy sources is one of the most transformative impacts of SF. Global economies have been propelled by fossil fuels, including coal, oil, and gas, for decades. However, their environmental impact—particularly in terms of carbon emissions—has led to a push for cleaner, more sustainable energy sources (Kalair *et al.*, 2021). This shift is not only driven by ethical considerations but also by economic logic. The geopolitics of renewable energy, noting that most literature emerged after 2010. While renewable energy offers benefits for global security, it also introduces risks related to critical materials and cybersecurity, with former fossil fuel exporters like Saudi Arabia and Russia expected to be the biggest losers in the energy transition. The literature is critiqued for lacking clear definitions and methodologies, with insufficient attention to coal-reliant countries such as Australia, China, Germany, Indonesia, Poland, and the United States (Vakulchuk *et al.*, 2020). However, the transition is not without challenges. Fossil fuel-dependent industries and regions face significant economic and social adjustments as jobs in the coal, oil, and gas sectors decline.

CASE STUDIES OF COUNTRIES WITH EFFECTIVE SF PRACTICES

Sustainable Finance (SF) has demonstrated its potential to drive economic growth, environmental sustainability, and social inclusion across a variety of contexts. While large economies like Germany and China have made notable strides, smaller and less-studied regions—especially in Africa and Latin America—also offer valuable insights into the transformative power of SF. The following cases illustrate this geographical diversity:

Germany stands as a leader in the global sustainable finance movement, especially through its ambitious “Energiewende” (energy transition) policy. This initiative has channeled significant investments into renewable energy sources such as wind and solar. Moreover, Germany has been a forerunner in green bond issuance, which has facilitated the country’s transition to a low-carbon economy.

These measures have contributed to substantial reductions in carbon emissions, the creation of green jobs, and increased national energy security (Germany 2020, 2020).

Despite facing scrutiny for high pollution levels, China has emerged as a global force in green finance. Government-led incentives have driven financial institutions to support environmentally sustainable projects, leading to rapid growth in the green bond market. By shifting from coal dependency to renewable energy sources, China is fostering both economic expansion and job creation (Urban *et al.*, 2016).

Costa Rica represents a compelling case from Latin America. The country has invested heavily in renewable energy—particularly geothermal, wind, and hydropower—which has allowed it to produce nearly all its electricity from renewable sources. With a national goal of becoming carbon neutral by 2050, Costa Rica exemplifies how strong political commitment paired with SF can yield significant environmental and economic gains (Green Business Benchmark, 2024).

Kenya has established itself as a trailblazer in sustainable finance within Africa. The country's geothermal energy initiatives, bolstered by international climate funds, have positioned it as a regional leader in clean energy. Furthermore, Kenya's pioneering use of fintech and mobile banking—such as M-Pesa—has advanced financial inclusion for millions. These strategies not only reduce environmental impact but also stimulate inclusive economic growth (Muhammad *et al.*, 2023).

As a small, less-studied country, Bhutan has integrated sustainable finance principles through its unique Gross National Happiness (GNH) framework, which prioritizes ecological conservation and well-being over GDP growth. Supported by international development finance, Bhutan has pursued green energy initiatives, particularly in hydropower, and environmental preservation strategies. Bhutan offers an alternative model for aligning finance with holistic development values.

In West Africa, Ghana has taken progressive steps by launching its own green bond framework aimed at attracting investment into sustainable infrastructure, agriculture, and energy projects. Though still at an early stage, Ghana's efforts demonstrate how smaller emerging economies can engage with SF to address development and environmental challenges simultaneously.

CHALLENGES AND RISKS IN SUSTAINABLE FINANCE

SF, while offering immense potential for fostering economic growth, environmental sustainability, and social equity, also presents several challenges and risks. This piece explores some of the major challenges, such as greenwashing, lack of transparency, limited availability of data on ESG metrics, the role of governments and financial institutions in overcoming these challenges, and the risk of fragmentation in regulatory approaches across different regions.

Greenwashing and Lack of Transparency

The practice of deceiving investors or customers by fraudulently marketing financial goods or projects as environmentally beneficial is known as "greenwashing," and it is one of the biggest issues facing the SF industry (Kaner, 2021). As SF becomes more popular, companies and financial institutions may be tempted to exaggerate their commitment to sustainability to attract investment, without making substantial changes to their business practices or operations.

Greenwashing undermines the integrity of SF by diluting the true impact of ESG-focused investments. Investors who believe they are contributing to positive environmental or social outcomes may find that their money is supporting businesses with minimal sustainability efforts or, worse, harmful environmental practices. This can result in reputational damage for the SF sector and a loss of trust among investors and stakeholders. Moreover, the lack of transparency in ESG reporting exacerbates the problem. Without clear, standardized disclosure requirements, companies can selectively report their sustainability performance in a way that paints an overly positive picture. This lack of transparency makes it difficult for investors to accurately assess the ESG credentials of companies and funds, increasing the risk of unintentional greenwashing (Yu *et al.*, 2020). Several high-profile cases of greenwashing have surfaced in recent years, with companies accused of overstating their environmental commitments or failing to deliver on promised sustainability targets. These instances have drawn increased scrutiny from regulators and stakeholders, highlighting the urgent need for stronger standards, verification processes, and penalties for greenwashing.

Limited Availability of Data on ESG Metrics

The availability and quality of data on ESG metrics remain major challenges in SF. ESG factors, which cover a wide range of issues such as carbon emissions, labour practices, diversity, and board governance, are crucial for investors to assess the sustainability and ethical impact of their investments (Keeley *et al.*, 2022). However, gathering reliable, consistent, and comparable data on ESG metrics is complex and often inconsistent across industries, regions, and companies.

The absence of standardised reporting frameworks for ESG data is a significant issue. Organisations such as the Sustainability Accounting Standards Board (SASB), Global Reporting Initiative (GRI), and the Task Force on Climate-related Financial Disclosures (TCFD) have provided guidelines, but there is still no globally accepted standard for ESG reporting. Despite this, some progress has been made. This fragmentation leads to a lack of uniformity in the manner in which companies report on ESG issues, which complicates the process of comparative performance across companies or industries for investors. In addition, many companies—especially smaller firms—lack the resources or expertise to accurately track and report on ESG metrics. This results in data gaps, where critical information about a company's environmental or social impact is either missing or incomplete. For investors looking to integrate ESG factors into their decision-making, these data limitations pose significant challenges.

The Role of Governments and Financial Institutions in Overcoming Challenges

Governments and financial institutions play a critical role in addressing the challenges facing SF. By setting clear standards, providing incentives, and promoting transparency, they can help ensure the long-term success and credibility of the sector.

Governments can address greenwashing and the lack of transparency by implementing robust regulations and disclosure requirements for companies and financial institutions. Several countries and regions have already made substantial progress in this regard. This regulation aims to combat greenwashing by providing investors with greater clarity on the sustainability credentials of their investments. Governments can also promote the standardization of ESG data by supporting the development of common reporting frameworks and encouraging businesses to adopt them. This could involve mandating ESG reporting for publicly listed companies or providing tax incentives for businesses that demonstrate strong ESG performance.

Additionally, governments can help mobilize private capital for SF by creating favorable regulatory environments, providing subsidies or tax breaks for green investments, and offering guarantees to reduce the risks associated with investing in new or unproven sustainable technologies. Financial institutions can contribute to the allocation of capital to initiatives that are truly sustainable by incorporating ESG factors into their risk assessment and decision-making processes. Collaboration between governments and financial institutions is also essential for overcoming challenges in SF. Public-private partnerships, where governments provide financial support or de-risking mechanisms for sustainable projects, can help scale up investments in areas such as renewable energy, energy efficiency, and sustainable agriculture. The implementation of Indonesia's SF roadmap highlights procedural compliance by financial institutions, but has inconsistencies in defining 'green' projects, leading to token efforts. For example, financial institutions submit sustainability reports but vary in interpreting green investments (Setyowati, 2023).

Risk of Fragmentation in Regulatory Approaches Across Regions

A significant challenge in the SF sector is the risk of fragmentation in regulatory approaches across different regions (Fransen & Conzelmann, 2015). While SF is a global issue, regulatory frameworks and policies often vary widely between countries and regions, creating inconsistencies and barriers for investors and companies operating across borders.

For example, the European Union has been a pioneer in SF, enacting regulations such as the SFDR and the EU Taxonomy, a classification system that identifies which economic activities are environmentally sustainable. (Cremasco & Boni, 2024). However, other regions, such as the United States and Asia, have been slower to implement similar regulations, leading to a patchwork of rules and standards that can be difficult for global companies and investors to navigate. The lack of harmonization between regulatory approaches poses several risks. First, it creates confusion and inefficiencies for companies and financial institutions that operate in multiple jurisdictions. They may be required to comply with different ESG reporting standards, which increases compliance costs and complexity. Investors seeking to allocate capital to sustainable projects may struggle to identify opportunities in markets with weaker or less transparent ESG regulations, limiting the flow of capital to critical areas such as climate change mitigation and social development. The risk of fragmentation is particularly concerning as global supply chains are increasingly interconnected, and many of the sustainability challenges, such as climate change, are inherently global in nature. Without coordinated action and consistent regulatory standards, efforts to address these challenges may be undermined by regulatory arbitrage, where companies or investors shift activities to regions with weaker environmental or social standards. This risk is being addressed by the increasing necessity for international collaboration in the field of science fiction. The promotion of global standards for SF and the encouragement of countries to align their regulatory frameworks can be facilitated by multilateral organisations, including the United Nations, the World Bank, and the International Monetary Fund (IMF). In the same vein, regional organisations such as the European Union and the Association of

Southeast Asian Nations (ASEAN) can collaborate to harmonise policies within their respective regions, thereby ensuring that investors are provided with a higher degree of consistency and clarity (Jusoh *et al.*, 2019).

However, the sector faces significant challenges, including greenwashing, lack of transparency, limited availability of ESG data, and the risk of regulatory fragmentation across regions. Governments and financial institutions must work together to overcome these obstacles by implementing robust standards, promoting transparency, and fostering international cooperation. By addressing these challenges, SF can continue to grow and deliver meaningful environmental, social, and economic benefits for the global economy.

THE FUTURE OF SUSTAINABLE FINANCE

Looking to the future, emerging trends, demographic shifts, technological advancements, and innovative financial instruments will continue to transform the landscape of SF. This article explores the future of SF by highlighting emerging trends, the role of younger generations, the potential of digital currencies, policy recommendations for scaling SF, and the transformative impact of innovation.

Emerging Trends: Circular Economy Finance, Blue Bonds, and Climate Resilience Funds

One of the most exciting aspects of the future of SF is the rise of circular economy finance. Unlike the traditional linear economic model, which is based on "take, make, dispose," the circular economy emphasizes minimizing waste, reusing materials, and creating sustainable business cycles. Financing the transition to a circular economy involves supporting businesses that focus on resource efficiency, recycling, and sustainable production. As more companies recognize the value of sustainable practices, circular economy finance is likely to grow, offering new investment opportunities that align with social and economic goals.

Another emerging trend is the introduction of blue bonds, which finance projects that support the sustainable use of ocean resources, marine conservation, and coastal protection (Thompson, 2022). Given that oceans play a critical role in regulating the Earth's climate and providing livelihoods for millions, blue bonds are set to become an essential tool in the fight against marine pollution and overfishing. The Seychelles was the first country to issue blue bonds in 2018, raising $15 million to fund marine conservation and sustainable fisheries (World Bank Group, 2018). The success of such initiatives indicates that blue bonds could have a growing role in protecting marine ecosystems while offering financial returns.

The future of SF is also expected to be influenced by climate resilience funds. These funds concentrate on the financing of projects that assist communities and businesses in adapting to the effects of climate change, including protracted droughts, extreme weather events, and rising sea levels. (Bracking & Leffel, 2021). Investing in infrastructure that is climate-resilient, such as flood defences and drought-resistant crops, will not only mitigate climate risks but also contribute to long-term economic stability. As climate risks continue to intensify, these funds will become increasingly important for safeguarding vulnerable populations and promoting SD.

The Role of Millennials and Gen Z in Driving the Sustainability Agenda

The future of SF is closely tied to the growing influence of Millennials and Gen Z, who are driving the global sustainability agenda. These younger generations are more conscious of social, environmental, and ethical issues than their predecessors, and their preferences are shaping the way businesses and financial institutions operate (Dabija *et al.*, 2019). Millennials and Gen Z are increasingly prioritising investments that are consistent with their values, with a significant number of them choosing impact investing or ESG funds. Studies show that younger investors are more likely to consider sustainability when making financial decisions, seeking out companies that demonstrate strong ESG performance. This shift is prompting financial institutions to offer more sustainable investment products and to integrate ESG factors into their investment strategies.

In addition, the younger generations are demanding greater transparency and accountability from companies. They are pushing for businesses to report their environmental impact, supply chain practices, and corporate governance policies in a more detailed and transparent manner. As a result, SF is likely to be shaped by a demand for better ESG reporting standards and enhanced scrutiny of corporate sustainability claims. Millennials and Gen Z are also influencing consumer behavior by supporting sustainable brands and products. As these generations continue to increase their wealth and market influence, their emphasis on sustainability will further drive the expansion of SF.

Potential for Digital Currencies in Financing Sustainability

Digital currencies, particularly Central Bank Digital Currencies (CBDCs) and cryptocurrencies, have the potential to revolutionize the financing of sustainable initiatives. As digital currencies become more prevalent, they could provide new avenues for funding sustainability projects, particularly in emerging markets and regions with underdeveloped financial systems (Thaker *et al.*, 2022). One potential benefit of digital currencies is their ability to increase financial inclusion. By reducing the reliance on traditional banking systems, digital currencies can provide access to financial services for unbanked populations, making it easier for them to participate in the global economy and support sustainable initiatives. For example, blockchain technology could be used to create decentralized platforms that connect investors directly with sustainable projects, eliminating intermediaries and reducing transaction costs.

Moreover, digital currencies can facilitate transparent and traceable financial transactions, which is crucial for ensuring that funds are used for their intended sustainable purposes. Blockchain technology can enable the tracking of funds from donors or investors to specific sustainability projects, reducing the risk of misallocation or corruption. This transparency is likely to attract more investors who want assurance that their funds are contributing to genuine sustainability efforts.

However, the sustainability of cryptocurrencies themselves is still a matter of debate. The environmental impact of cryptocurrency mining, particularly for energy-intensive coins like Bitcoin, has raised concerns. To mitigate this, the future of digital currencies in SF may rely on the development of eco-friendly cryptocurrencies that utilize more energy-efficient consensus mechanisms, such as proof-of-stake, or by transitioning to renewable energy sources for mining operations.

Policy Recommendations for Scaling Sustainable Finance

To accelerate the growth and effectiveness of Sustainable Finance (SF), governments, regulators, and international bodies must adopt targeted, actionable policies that reduce barriers, increase investor confidence, and promote global equity. The following refined recommendations outline specific measures that can make SF more impactful and scalable:

1. Harmonize and Enforce Standardized ESG Reporting Frameworks

Governments should work with international organizations such as the International Sustainability Standards Board (ISSB), Global Reporting Initiative (GRI), and Task Force on Climate-related Financial Disclosures (TCFD) to adopt unified ESG reporting standards. A legally binding ESG reporting framework—tailored for both public and private companies—should be implemented across sectors, with sector-specific disclosure templates and third-party audit mechanisms to ensure consistency, comparability, and credibility of sustainability data.

Actionable Step: Create regional ESG compliance bodies under national financial regulators to monitor disclosure quality and provide technical assistance to reporting entities.

2. Introduce Harmonized Tax Incentives for Green Bonds and Sustainable Assets

Governments should introduce clear, consistent tax relief mechanisms (*e.g.*, tax deductions, zero capital gains tax) for certified green bonds and sustainable infrastructure investments. Establishing national-level green bond standards, aligned with ICMA's Green Bond Principles, will attract institutional investors and ensure the integrity of labeled products.

Actionable Step: Develop a "Green Investment Taxonomy" that defines eligible projects and sectors, streamlining access to fiscal incentives and preventing greenwashing.

3. Mandate Climate Risk Disclosure with Clear Metrics

Financial regulators should require firms—especially those in carbon-intensive sectors—to disclose climate-related risks using scenario analysis, carbon footprint metrics, and climate Value-at-Risk (VaR). These disclosures should include both transition risks (*e.g.*, policy shifts, market shifts) and physical risks (*e.g.*, climate-related asset damage).

Actionable Step: Require listed companies to file climate risk disclosures as part of their annual financial reports, following TCFD-aligned templates, and provide training to company boards on interpreting and managing climate risk.

4. Scale Up Climate Finance for Developing Countries through Coordinated International Mechanisms

International Financial Institutions (IFIs) and donor countries should expand concessional finance facilities and guarantees to de-risk green projects in emerging economies. Enhanced funding should prioritize adaptation, community resilience, and renewable energy access in vulnerable regions.

Actionable Step: Create a blended finance platform under the Green Climate Fund (GCF) that combines public funds with private capital to co-finance high-impact projects in Least Developed Countries (LDCs), offering interest rate buy-downs or partial risk guarantees.

5. Promote Sustainable Public Procurement and Government-Led Green Financing

Governments can lead by example through green procurement mandates, issuing sovereign green bonds, and establishing national climate funds to co-invest with the private sector in strategic projects such as clean energy, climate-smart agriculture, and resilient infrastructure.

Actionable Step: Set national targets for green procurement (*e.g.*, 30% of government contracts by 2030) and publish annual progress reports to drive accountability and transparency.

HOW INNOVATION WILL CONTINUE TO TRANSFORM SUSTAINABLE FINANCE

Innovation will remain a key driver of transformation in the SF sector. As new technologies, financial instruments, and business models emerge, they will create new opportunities for scaling sustainability efforts and improving financial outcomes.

One area where innovation is likely to have a significant impact is fintech (financial technology). Fintech companies are already creating new platforms that allow individuals and institutions to invest directly in sustainable projects, bypassing traditional financial intermediaries. These platforms are improving access to capital for small and medium-sized enterprises (SMEs) engaged in sustainability initiatives, which may otherwise struggle to secure financing from conventional sources. AI and machine learning will alter SF alongside fintech. AI can analyse massive ESG data to find patterns, hazards, and opportunities that conventional research may miss. This might help investors make better judgments and fund sustainable initiatives. Finally, sustainability-linked bonds and climate transition bonds will grow. These products allow investors to achieve environmental objectives while earning money. Financial markets will innovate to fund the transition to a more sustainable global economy as green investment demand develops.

The future of SF will be shaped by emerging trends such as circular economy finance, blue bonds, and climate resilience funds, as well as the growing influence of Millennials and Gen Z. Digital currencies have the potential to play a pivotal role in financing sustainability, while policy reforms and innovations will help scale SF efforts. By continuing to adapt and evolve, SF will remain a powerful tool for addressing global challenges and promoting long-term economic and environmental stability.

CASE STUDIES

Germany: Commerzbank's Green Finance Leadership

Commerzbank, one of Germany's leading financial institutions, has been at the forefront of sustainable finance initiatives. The bank has issued green bonds totaling €1.5 billion to fund renewable energy projects and has implemented strict policies to phase out coal financing. In 2022, Commerzbank became the first German bank to have its interim 2030 carbon reduction targets validated by the Science Based Targets initiative (SBTi), aligning its portfolio with the goals of the Paris Agreement. The bank also supports the German Sustainability Code and has committed to using only renewable electricity for its operations in Germany since 2013.

China: Ant Forest's Digital Green Finance Innovation

Ant Forest, launched by Ant Financial (an affiliate of Alibaba), is a pioneering digital platform that gamifies carbon footprint reduction. Users earn "green energy" points through eco-friendly activities, which are then used to plant real trees in arid regions of China. As of the end of 2022, over 650 million users participated, leading to the planting of more than 100 million trees and a reduction of over 26 million tons of carbon emissions. This initiative demonstrates how digital finance can engage the public in sustainability efforts at scale.

Kenya: M-KOPA Solar's Pay-As-You-Go Model

M-KOPA Solar is a Kenyan-based company that provides affordable solar home systems to off-grid households through a pay-as-you-go model. Customers make small, incremental payments *via* mobile money platforms until they fully own the solar systems. This approach has enabled over a million households in Kenya, Uganda, and Tanzania to access clean energy, reducing reliance on fossil fuels and improving living standards. M-KOPA's model exemplifies how innovative financing can overcome barriers to renewable energy access in underserved communities.

Emerging Trends in Sustainable Finance

1. Circular Economy Finance

Circular economy finance refers to investment mechanisms that support resource efficiency, recycling, and regenerative economic models, moving away from the traditional linear "take-make-dispose" paradigm. Financial organizations are progressively designing products that help firms engaged in remanufacturing, recycling, and circular supply chains (OECD, 2020). The European Investment Bank (EIB) has commercialised targeted instruments for circular economy ventures, including waste-to-energy and product life-extension financing (EIB, 2021). For instance, ING Group has developed a "circular economy scorecard" for evaluating client projects and provides preferential financing terms to companies that achieve high circularity metrics (ING, 2021).

2. Blue Bonds

Blue bonds are innovative debt instruments that finance ocean-related projects such as sustainable fisheries, coral reef restoration, and marine biodiversity protection. These bonds emerged following the successful issuance of the Seychelles' Blue Bond in 2018, which raised $15 million to support sustainable marine and fisheries projects (World Bank, 2019). Since then, interest has grown, particularly in small island developing states (SIDS) and coastal economies. For instance, in 2022, the Asian Development Bank (ADB) issued a $50 million blue bond to support marine ecosystem resilience in the Pacific, marking a significant commitment to ocean health (ADB, 2022).

3. Transition Finance

Transition finance focuses on funding for high-emitting sectors (*e.g.*, steel, cement, aviation) to help them shift towards low-carbon operations. This approach is gaining traction as part of the "just transition" framework, which ensures that economic shifts toward sustainability also promote social equity and labor protection (OECD, 2022).

4. Sustainability-Linked Bonds (SLBs)

Unlike green or blue bonds, which are project-specific, SLBs tie bond performance to company-wide ESG targets. If the issuer fails to meet predefined sustainability KPIs (*e.g.*, CO_2 reduction), they must pay a penalty through higher interest rates. SLBs offer flexible use-of-proceeds but maintain strong sustainability accountability (ICMA, 2023).

5. Nature-Based Finance

This trend aligns finance with biodiversity goals, including investments in reforestation, wetlands, and carbon sinks. The Taskforce on Nature-related Financial Disclosures (TNFD) has been pushing for standards to help investors assess nature-related risks and opportunities (TNFD, 2023).

CONCLUSION

Sustainable finance emphasises government, financial, and corporate partnerships to solve global environmental, social, and economic issues. SF, though facing significant hurdles such as greenwashing, fragmented regulations, and limited reliable ESG data, holds immense potential for creating a more resilient and equitable global economy. The discussion highlighted the importance of overcoming these challenges and recognized emerging trends such as circular economy finance, blue bonds, and climate resilience funds, which present innovative ways to finance sustainability efforts. Millennials and Gen Z are also pushing the sustainability agenda forward, demanding transparency and driving the integration of ESG factors into investment strategies. Digital currencies and blockchain technology, which offer enhanced transparency and financial inclusion, can further revolutionize SF. Additionally, the importance of policy measures to standardize ESG reporting and incentivize green investments is critical to scaling the sector.

These emerging trends—circular economy finance, blue bonds, transition instruments, SLBs, and nature-based finance—highlight the rapid evolution and increasing sophistication of the sustainable finance ecosystem. These innovations broaden the scope of SF beyond carbon metrics, addressing systemic ecological, economic, and social challenges in an integrated manner. SF has a bright future as AI, big data analytics, and blockchain increase ESG research and transparency. The growing demand for ESG-focused investments is also pushing companies to align with ethical considerations, while climate change mitigation and adaptation will drive increased investment in renewable energy and climate-resilient infrastructure. Furthermore, the integration of social and governance factors will become more prominent as investors hold companies accountable for diversity, inclusion, labour rights, and governance practices. To unlock the full potential of SF, stakeholders must embrace technological innovation, promote financial inclusion, raise awareness about the benefits of ESG integration, and prioritize long-term thinking over short-term profits. Through international collaboration and a commitment to sustainability, SF can become a driving force for global development, supporting both economic growth and environmental stewardship.

REFERENCES

Aceleanu, M.I. (2015). Green jobs in a green economy: support for a sustainable development. *Progress in Industrial Ecology, an International Journal, 9*(4), 341.
[http://dx.doi.org/10.1504/PIE.2015.076894]

Alonso, S.L.N. (2023). Can Central Bank Digital Currencies be green and sustainable? *Green Finance, 5*(4), 603-623.
[http://dx.doi.org/10.3934/GF.2023023]

Alshehhi, A., Nobanee, H., Khare, N. (2018). The impact of sustainability practices on corporate financial performance: Literature trends and future research potential. *Sustainability (Basel), 10*(2), 494. [http://dx.doi.org/10.3390/su10020494]

Banga, J. (2019). The green bond market: a potential source of climate finance for developing countries. *Journal of Sustainable Finance & Investment, 9*(1), 17-32. [http://dx.doi.org/10.1080/20430795.2018.1498617]

Battiston, S., Dafermos, Y., Monasterolo, I. (2021). Climate risks and financial stability. *J. Financ. Stab., 54*(100867), 100867. [http://dx.doi.org/10.1016/j.jfs.2021.100867]

Belinky, A., Saraiva, M.H., Miyake, A. (2022). Challenges to current sustainability assessment frameworks: The era of Big Data and SDGs has arrived. *Int. J. Soc. Ecol. Sustain. Dev., 13*(6), 1-14. [http://dx.doi.org/10.4018/IJSESD.301248]

Bracking, S., Leffel, B. (2021). Climate finance governance: Fit for purpose? *Wiley Interdiscip. Rev. Clim. Change, 12*(4), e709. [http://dx.doi.org/10.1002/wcc.709]

Calandra, D., Secinaro, S., Massaro, M., Dal Mas, F., Bagnoli, C. (2023). The link between sustainable business models and Blockchain: A multiple case study approach. *Bus. Strategy Environ., 32*(4), 1403-1417. [http://dx.doi.org/10.1002/bse.3195]

Christiansen, A.C., Wettestad, J. (2003). The EU as a frontrunner on greenhouse gas emissions trading: how did it happen and will the EU succeed? *Climate Policy, 3*(1), 3-18. [http://dx.doi.org/10.3763/cpol.2003.0302]

Green Business Benchmark. (2024). *Costa Rica's path to sustainability: A pioneer in Latin America.* https://www.greenbusinessbenchmark.com/archive/costa-rica-sustainability .

Cremasco, C., Boni, L. (2024). Is the European Union (EU) Sustainable Finance Disclosure Regulation (SFDR) effective in shaping sustainability objectives? An analysis of investment funds' behaviour. *Journal of Sustainable Finance & Investment, 14*(4), 1018-1036. [http://dx.doi.org/10.1080/20430795.2022.2124838]

Dabija, D.-C., Bejan, B. M., & Dinu, V. (2019). How sustainability oriented is Generation Z in retail? A literature review. *Transformations in Business & Economics,* 18(2), 140..

Cristina, D., Florina, B., Carmen-Valentina, R. (2023). Green investments: Opportunities for sustainable economic growth. *Annals of Dunarea de Jos University of Galati Fascicle I Economics and Applied Informatics, 29*(3), 95-101. [http://dx.doi.org/10.35219/eai15840409367]

Dorfleitner, G., & Braun, D. (2019). Fintech, digitalization and blockchain: Possible applications for green finance. In *Palgrave studies in impact finance* (pp. 207–237). Springer International Publishing..

Edmans, A., Kacperczyk, M. (2022). Sustainable Finance. *Review of Finance, 26*(6), 1309-1313. [http://dx.doi.org/10.1093/rof/rfac069]

Fatemi, A.M., Fooladi, I.J. (2013). Sustainable finance: A new paradigm. *Global Finance Journal, 24*(2), 101-113. [http://dx.doi.org/10.1016/j.gfj.2013.07.006]

Fransen, L., Conzelmann, T. (2015). Fragmented or cohesive transnational private regulation of sustainability standards? A comparative study. *Regulation & Governance, 9*(3), 259-275. [http://dx.doi.org/10.1111/rego.12055]

Fraser, A., Tan, S., Lagarde, M., Mays, N. (2018). Narratives of promise, narratives of caution: A review of the literature on social impact bonds. *Social Policy and Administration, 52*(1), 4-28. [http://dx.doi.org/10.1111/spol.12260]

Friede, G., Busch, T., Bassen, A. (2015). ESG and financial performance: aggregated evidence from more than 2000 empirical studies. *Journal of Sustainable Finance & Investment, 5*(4), 210-233.

[http://dx.doi.org/10.1080/20430795.2015.1118917]

International Energy Agency. (2020, February 19). *Germany 2020.* Available from: https://www.iea.org/reports/germany-2020.

Climate Policy Initiative. (2019, November 7). *Global landscape of climate finance 2019.* https://www.climatepolicyinitiative.org/publication/global-landscape-of-climate-finance-2019/.

Gomber, P., Kauffman, R.J., Parker, C., Weber, B.W. (2018). On the fintech revolution: Interpreting the forces of innovation, disruption, and transformation in financial services. *Journal of Management Information Systems, 35*(1), 220-265.
[http://dx.doi.org/10.1080/07421222.2018.1440766]

Hogarth, J. (2012). The role of climate finance in innovation systems. *Journal of SF & Investment, 2*(3–4), 257-274.
[http://dx.doi.org/10.1080/20430795.2012.74263]

Hou, T.C.T. (2019). The relationship between corporate social responsibility and sustainable financial performance: firm-level evidence from Taiwan. *Corporate Social Responsibility and Environmental Management, 26*(1), 19-28.
[http://dx.doi.org/10.1002/csr.1647]

Hussain, S., Rasheed, A., Rehman, S. (2023). Driving sustainable growth: exploring the link between financial innovation, green finance and sustainability performance: banking evidence. *Kybernetes, 53*(11), 4678-4696.
[http://dx.doi.org/10.1108/K-05-2023-0918]

International Labour Organization (2018, May 14) *24 million jobs to open up in the green economy* Available from: https://www.ilo.org/resource/news/24-million-jobs-open-green-economy-0

Ionescu, L. (2021). Corporate environmental performance, climate change mitigation, and green innovation behavior in sustainable finance. *Economics Management and Financial Markets, 16*(3), 94-106. Available from: https://www.ceeol.com/search/article-detail?id=983519

Jusoh, S., Ramli, I.M., Damuri, Y.R. (2019). Regional regulatory coherence in the association of southeast Asian nation: The case of competition law and intellectual property. *Eria.org.* Available from: https://www.eria.org/uploads/media/11.AV2040_VOL4_Regional_Regulatory_Coherence.pdf

Kalair, A., Abas, N., Saleem, M.S., Kalair, A.R., Khan, N. (2021). Role of energy storage systems in energy transition from fossil fuels to renewables. *Energy Storage, 3*(1), e135.
[http://dx.doi.org/10.1002/est2.135]

Kaner, G. (2021). Greenwashing: How difficult it is to be transparent to the consumer—H&M case study. In Palgrave Studies of Marketing in Emerging Economies (pp. 203–226). Springer International Publishing..

Keeley, A.R., Chapman, A.J., Yoshida, K., Xie, J., Imbulana, J., Takeda, S., Managi, S. (2022). ESG metrics and social equity: Investigating commensurability. *Frontiers in Sustainability, 3*, 920955.
[http://dx.doi.org/10.3389/frsus.2022.920955]

Kwilinski, A., Lyulyov, O., Pimonenko, T. (2023). Greenfield investment as a catalyst of green economic growth. *Energies, 16*(5), 2372.
[http://dx.doi.org/10.3390/en16052372]

Lopez-de-Silanes, F., McCahery, J.A., Pudschedl, P.C. (2024). Institutional investors and ESG preferences. *Corporate Governance, 32*(6), 1060-1086.
[http://dx.doi.org/10.1111/corg.12583]

Macchiavello, E., Siri, M. (2022). Sustainable finance and Fintech: Can technology contribute to achieving environmental goals? A preliminary assessment of 'Green Fintech' and 'sustainable Digital Finance.'. *European Company and Financial Law Review, 19*(1), 128-174.
[http://dx.doi.org/10.1515/ecfr-2022-0005]

Maltais, A., Nykvist, B. (2020). Understanding the role of green bonds in advancing sustainability. *Journal of*

Sustainable Finance & Investment.
[http://dx.doi.org/10.1080/20430795.2020.1724864]

Mervelskemper, L., Kaltofen, D., Stein, S. (2014). Are sustainable investment funds worth the effort? *Journal of Sustainable Finance & Investment, 4*(2), 127-146.
[http://dx.doi.org/10.1080/20430795.2013.837809]

Mocanu, M., Constantin, L.G., Cernat-Gruici, B. (2021). Sustainability bonds. An international event study. *The Journal of Business Economics and Management, 22*(6), 1551-1576.
[http://dx.doi.org/10.3846/jbem.2021.15372]

Muhammad, A., Ibitomi, T., Durotimi Amos, D., Idris, M.B., Ishaq, A.A. (2023). Comparative analysis of sustainable finance initiatives in Asia and Africa: A path towards global sustainability. *Global Sustainability Research, 2*(3), 33-51.
[http://dx.doi.org/10.56556/gssr.v2i3.559]

Musleh Al-Sartawi, A. M. A., Hussainey, K., Razzaque, A. (2022). The role of artificial intelligence in sustainable finance. *Journal of Sustainable Finance & Investment,* 1-6.
[http://dx.doi.org/10.1080/20430795.2022.2057405]

Narassimhan, E., Gallagher, K.S., Koester, S., Alejo, J.R. (2018). Carbon pricing in practice: a review of existing emissions trading systems. *Climate Policy, 18*(8), 967-991.
[http://dx.doi.org/10.1080/14693062.2018.1467827]

Ostojić, I., Petrović, P., Kelić, V. (2024). Blended finance as a sustainable development support mechanism. In *Legal insights into environmental sustainability (pp. 170–194). Institut društvenih nauka.*

Pasi, G. (2014). Challenges for European welfare systems. A research agenda on social impact bonds. *Review of Applied Socio-Economic Research, 8*, 141-150. Available from: https://reaser.eu/RePec/rse/wpaper/REASER8_16Pasi_P141-150.pdf

Qin, M., Su, C.W., Zhong, Y., Song, Y., Lobonţ, O.R. (2022). Sustainable finance and renewable energy: Promoters of carbon neutrality in the United States. *Journal of Environmental Management, 324*(116390), 116390.
[http://dx.doi.org/10.1016/j.jenvman.2022.116390] [PMID: 36352713]

Ren, Y.S., Ma, C.Q., Chen, X.Q., Lei, Y.T., Wang, Y.R. (2023). Sustainable finance and blockchain: A systematic review and research agenda. *Research in International Business and Finance, 64*(101871), 101871.
[http://dx.doi.org/10.1016/j.ribaf.2022.101871]

International Renewable Energy Agency. (2020, September 29). *Renewable energy jobs continue growth to 11.5 million worldwide.*
https://www.irena.org/news/pressreleases/2020/Sep/Renewable-Energy-Jobs-Continue-Growth--o-11-5-Million-Worldwide.

Sadati, A., Gramlich, D., Walker, T. (2024). Artificial intelligence, finance, and sustainability: An overview. *In Artificial Intelligence, Finance, and Sustainability* (pp. 3-16). Springer Nature Switzerland.

Saxena, A., Ramaswamy, M., Beale, J., Marciniuk, D., Smith, P. (2021). Striving for the United Nations (UN) Sustainable Development Goals (SDGs): what will it take? *Discover Sustainability, 2*(1), 20.
[http://dx.doi.org/10.1007/s43621-021-00029-8]

Setyowati, A.B. (2023). Governing sustainable finance: insights from Indonesia. *Climate Policy, 23*(1), 108-121.
[http://dx.doi.org/10.1080/14693062.2020.1858741]

Su, E. (2018). *Exchange-traded funds (ETFs): Issues for Congress* (CRS Report No. R45318). Congressional Research Service. https://sgp.fas.org/crs/misc/R45318.pdf.

Thaker, M.A.B.M.T., Khaliq, A.B., Thaker, H.B.M.T., Amin, M.F.B., Pitchay, A.B.A. (2022). The potential role of fintech and digital currency for Islamic green financing: Toward an integrated model. In: *Economics, Law, and Institutions in Asia Pacific.* Springer Nature.Singapore:

Thompson, B.S. (2022). Blue bonds for marine conservation and a sustainable ocean economy: Status, trends, and insights from green bonds. *Marine Policy, 144*(105219), 105219. [http://dx.doi.org/10.1016/j.marpol.2022.105219]

Tolliver, C., Fujii, H., Keeley, A.R., Managi, S. (2021). Green innovation and finance in Asia. *Asian Economic Policy Review, 16*(1), 67-87. [http://dx.doi.org/10.1111/aepr.12320]

Udeagha, M.C., Ngepah, N. (2023). The drivers of environmental sustainability in BRICS economies: Do green finance and fintech matter? *World Development Sustainability, 3*(100096), 100096. [http://dx.doi.org/10.1016/j.wds.2023.100096]

Urban, F., Geall, S., Wang, Y. (2016). Solar PV and solar water heaters in China: Different pathways to low carbon energy. *Renewable and Sustainable Energy Reviews, 64*, 531-542. [http://dx.doi.org/10.1016/j.rser.2016.06.023]

Vakulchuk, R., Overland, I., Scholten, D. (2020). Renewable energy and geopolitics: A review. *Renewable and Sustainable Energy Reviews, 122*(109547), 109547. [http://dx.doi.org/10.1016/j.rser.2019.109547]

Van de Velde, E., Vermeir, W., Corten, F. (2005). Corporate social responsibility and financial performance. *Corporate Governance (Bradford), 5*(3), 129-138. [http://dx.doi.org/10.1108/14720700510604760]

World Bank Group. (2018, October 29). *Seychelles launches world's first sovereign blue bond.* https://www.worldbank.org/en/news/press-release/2018/10/29/seychelles-launches-words-f-rst-sovereign-blue-bond.

Yu, E.P., Luu, B.V., Chen, C.H. (2020). Greenwashing in environmental, social and governance disclosures. *Research in International Business and Finance, 52*(101192), 101192. [http://dx.doi.org/10.1016/j.ribaf.2020.101192]

Ziolo, M., Bak, I., Cheba, K. (2020). The role of sustainable finance in achieving Sustainable Development Goals: Does it work? *Technological and Economic Development of Economy, 27*(1), 45-70. [http://dx.doi.org/10.3846/tede.2020.13863]

Ziolo, M., Fidanoski, F., Simeonovski, K., Filipovski, V., Jovanovska, K. (2017). Sustainable finance role in creating conditions for sustainable economic growth and development. *World Sustainability Series.* Springer International Publishing.

CHAPTER 6

Financial Development and Environmental sustainability: An Empirical Analysis of Major Asian Economies

Javid Ahmad Khan[1,*], **Mudasir Ahmad Sheergujree**[1] and **Sayed Gulzar Ganai**[2]

[1] *Department of Economics, Islamic University of Science and Technology (IUST), Awantipora, Jammu and Kashmir, India*

[2] *Department of Economics, Symbiosis International University, Pune, Maharashtra, India*

Abstract: The rapid economic growth in Asia, driven by technological advancements, manufacturing, and a significant population, has profound implications for environmental quality. This study investigates how financial development impacts environmental quality in major Asian economies—China, Japan, India, South Korea, and Indonesia—controlling for economic growth, human capital, and urbanization from 1990 to 2019. Utilizing the ARDL bounds testing approach, the analysis explores both short- and long-term relationships among these variables. Results indicate that financial development and urbanization contribute to increased CO_2 emissions in the long run, while rising GDP per capita tends to reduce emissions, likely due to cleaner technology adoption in advanced economies. However, human capital shows a positive association with emissions, underscoring the need for education focused on environmental sustainability. These findings emphasize the importance of policies promoting sustainable finance, green skill development, and clean technology adoption, supporting economic growth without compromising environmental health in Asia's rapidly developing economies.

Keywords: Asian economies, Clean technology adoption, Environmental sustainability, Financial development, Green skill development, Sustainable finance.

INTRODUCTION

Asia, with 59.05% of the global population, stands as a pivotal force in the global economy, with several of its economies ranking among the world's most significant in GDP. These Asian economies, especially the top five—China,

* **Corresponding author Javid Ahmad Khan:** Department of Economics, Islamic University of Science and Technology (IUST), Awantipora, Jammu and Kashmir, India; E-mail: javid.khan@iust.ac.in

Mohammed Majeed, Sofia Devi Shamurailatpam, Parag Sunil Shukla, Ibrahim Osman & Hamidu Gafaru Dokurugu (Eds.)

Japan, India, South Korea, and Indonesia—are integral to global economic dynamics due to their advancements in manufacturing, technology, and innovation. According to the 2024 World Population Review, China leads with an impressive GDP of $18.53 trillion, followed by Japan at $4.11 trillion, India at $3.94 trillion, South Korea at $1.76 trillion, and Indonesia at $1.48 trillion, as highlighted in the IMF's 2024 report. Asia's economic strength is further underscored by its financial development, marked by extensive market depth, access to financial services, and operational efficiency, which has facilitated this rapid growth trajectory.

However, the economic expansion of these nations has come at an environmental cost. The International Energy Agency's 2023 report indicates that global CO_2 emissions from energy use increased by 1.1%, reaching a record high of 37.4 billion tons, with China and India as leading contributors. This scenario underscores the critical importance of examining the relationship between economic growth and environmental sustainability in Asia, with a particular focus on the impact of financial development.

Historically, the financial sector's influence on economic growth has been extensively studied. Bagehot (1873) first recognized the crucial role of organized capital markets in promoting productive investments. Subsequently, scholars such as Schumpeter (1911), Hicks (1969), and Goldsmith (1969) emphasized that financial systems—particularly banking and capital markets—are instrumental in mobilizing savings and advancing technological innovation, which propel economic growth. The McKinnon-Shaw hypothesis (1973) further argued that financial liberalization is essential for economic growth, as restrictive policies such as high interest rates and credit controls, known as financial repression, limit financial development by discouraging savings and investments. In recent years, studies incorporating endogenous growth theory have demonstrated that financial systems play a key role in overcoming informational asymmetries between lenders and borrowers. Scholars such as Diamond (1984), Gale and Hellwig (1985), and King and Levine (1993) showed that financial institutions not only mobilize savings but also enhance resource allocation and investment monitoring, reducing risks and promoting sustained growth, especially in developing economies.

Nonetheless, the positive impacts of financial development are counterbalanced by its environmental implications. Financial expansion fuels industrial and manufacturing growth, often driven by high-emission energy sources, which aggravates environmental degradation. Research findings on this relationship are mixed: some studies indicate that financial growth and globalization exacerbate environmental harm (Zafar *et al.*, 2019), while others, such as Ahmad *et al.*

(2021), suggest that financial development can contribute to environmental sustainability. This study aims to analyze whether financial development in Asia's leading economies has not only propelled economic growth but also intensified energy demands and environmental challenges, shedding light on the complex dynamics between financial development, economic expansion, and environmental sustainability.

LITERATURE REVIEW

Exploring the nexus between Financial Development (FD) and Environmental Degradation (ED), existing literature reveals two primary linkages: the causative impact of financial development, which potentially worsens environmental conditions, and the deterrent role financial development may play in promoting sustainability. Scholars have examined this relationship from diverse perspectives, offering empirical evidence for both positive and negative impacts of FD on the environment. The first perspective sees financial development as a catalyst for environmental degradation. Many studies identify a direct link between increased financial development and worsening environmental conditions. Nawaz *et al.* (2020) and Alabi *et al.* (2021) argue that FD fuels economic activities leading to environmental harm, while Shahbaz *et al.* (2020a), Ali *et al.* (2019), and Hundie (2018) highlight that credit availability facilitates industrial growth, increasing non-renewable energy consumption and emissions. Alam (2022) and Rjoub *et al.* (2021) add that as financial markets develop, more capital becomes available for short-term economic investments, often at the cost of long-term environmental sustainability. Several regional studies reinforce this view: De Qiang *et al.* (2022) found that while financial inclusion boosts economic growth, it worsens environmental quality through increased carbon emissions in emerging economies from 2004 to 2019. Zu B. (2022) also links credit access to rising emissions. Ali *et al.* (2023) analyzed the E-7 countries, finding that high FD, rapid economic growth, and non-renewable energy use detract from environmental sustainability, recommending policies aligned with the UN's Sustainable Development Goals (SDGs). Similarly, Sethi *et al.* (2020), studying India (1980-2015), found that globalization and financial development degrade environmental quality, advocating for stringent regulations and green technology investments. Kirikkaleli *et al.* (2020) showed that while FD supports renewable energy use in the long term, economic growth often compromises environmental quality.

Conversely, a second body of literature presents financial development as potentially beneficial for environmental quality. This perspective suggests that FD can mitigate degradation if well-regulated. Creane *et al.* (2004) and Claessens and Feijen (2007) argue that financial development can channel investments toward sustainable initiatives, while Salahuddin *et al.* (2015) and Charfeddine and Kahia

(2019) indicate that FD can drive eco-friendly innovation and green finance, supporting a shift toward cleaner technologies. Khan *et al.* (2021) and Dasgupta *et al.* (2001) emphasize that, with policy support, FD can attract funds for renewable energy and efficient infrastructure. Some studies adopt a neutral stance, observing cases where FD neither worsens nor improves environmental degradation. For instance, Chen *et al.* (2019) found no significant evidence that FD alone impacts environmental quality in 16 Central and Eastern European countries (1980-2016). Xu *et al.* (2018) observed a similar neutrality in Saudi Arabia (1971-2016). For BRICS nations, Haseeb *et al.* (2018) found bidirectional causality between FD, CO_2 emissions, energy use, and growth, without clear evidence of FD's direct impact on environmental degradation. Finally, Asumadu-Sarkodie and Owusu (2016) reported that FD had no significant independent effect on environmental outcomes in Sri Lanka (1971-2012).

The existing literature thus reveals complex and varied findings on the FD-ED nexus, with diverse outcomes across regions and methodologies. This variability underscores the importance of context-specific policies and suggests that FD's impact on environmental sustainability may depend on regional economic conditions, regulatory environments, and the prioritization of green investments. However, research gaps remain in region-specific analyses, especially within emerging Asian economies, which are experiencing rapid financial growth, urbanization, and industrialization that distinctly impact environmental quality. This study addresses these gaps by examining the FD-ED link in leading emerging Asian economies, aiming to inform policy recommendations for sustainable growth in these rapidly developing regions.

METHODOLOGY AND THE EMPIRICAL FRAMEWORK

The role of financial development in economic growth is undeniably important, as it provides the necessary funding for sectors essential to an economy's progress. However, the critical question this study seeks to address is whether growth spurred by financial development can be achieved without compromising environmental quality. Focusing on emerging Asian economies, this study aims to quantify the impact of financial development on environmental degradation, specifically through the lens of carbon emissions as a measure of environmental quality. Based on previous research, we select carbon emissions as our dependent variable, with financial development as the independent variable, and include controls for economic growth, urbanization, and human capital, as these factors are highly relevant to emerging economies.

In line with recent studies (Hussian *et al.*, 2024; Saud *et al.*, 2020; Sethi *et al.*, 2020; Zu, 2022), we propose that carbon emissions led by financial development have a unidirectional relationship in the context of the conservation hypothesis in the top five Asian economies. By examining this relationship within the top five emerging Asian economies, this study seeks to provide insights that could guide policymakers in balancing financial growth with sustainability goals. The data used in this study were collected from the World Bank and Penn World. The description of variables and the sources of the data are presented in Table **1**. This study utilizes a comprehensive dataset covering China, Japan, India, South Korea, and Indonesia over the years 1990-2019.

Table 1. Description of variables.

Variable	Symbol	Description	Data Source
CO_2 Emissions	CO_2	CO_2 emissions (tons percapita)	World Development Indicators
Financial Development Index	FDI	Relative ranking of countries on the depth, access and efficiency of their financial institutions & markets.	International Monetary Fund
Gross Domestic product per capita	GDP	GDP Percapita constant 2015 US$	World Development Indicators
Human capital	HC	Human capital index based on years of Schooling	Penn World Table 10
Urban Population	URB	Proportion of urban population to the total Population	World Development Indicators

Source: Variables (World Bank).

This study employs a multi-framework model, incorporating an independent vector of human capital, growth, and urbanisation to robustly assess a comprehensive understanding of financial development's impact on Carbon emissions.

$$CO_2it = f(FDI_{it}, X_{it}) \tag{1}$$

Where,

CO_2it is Carbon emission, $FDI_{it}$is the Financial Development Index, and X_{it} is the vector of (GDP_{it}, $HCI_{it,}$ URB_{it}), where GDP represents growth, URB_{it} represents the Urbanization, and HCI is the human capital index. The vector X helps to overcome the problem of omitted variable bias.

The estimated empirical equation is represented as:

$$CO_2it = \beta_0 + \beta_1 FDI + \beta_2 GDP + \beta_3 HCI + \beta_4 URB + \varepsilon_t \tag{2}$$

Following Shahbaz *et al.* (2012), the log-linear specification of our empirical equation is modelled as follows

$$\ln CO_2 it = \beta_0 + \beta_1 \ln FDI + \beta_2 \ln GDP + \beta_3 LnHCI + \beta_4 \ln URB + \varepsilon_t \quad (3)$$

Augmented Dickey-Fuller (ADF) and Phillips-Perron (PP) unit root tests are used to examine the stationary properties for the long-run relationship of time series variables. The Augmented Dickey Fuller(ADF) test is based on the equation given below:

$$\Delta Y_t = \alpha_0 + \alpha_1 Y_{t-1} + \sum_{j-1}^{k} d_j \Delta Y_{tj} + \varepsilon_t \quad (4)$$

Where ε_t is a pure white noise error term, Δ is a difference operator, Y_t is a time series α_0, is the constant, and k is the optimum number of lags of the dependent variable. The Augmented Dickey Fuller (ADF) test determines whether the estimates of the coefficients are equal to zero. The ADF test provides the cumulative distribution of ADF Statistics. The variable is said to be stationary if the value of the coefficient δ is less than the critical values from the Fuller table. The Phillips-Perron (PP) unit root test equation is given below:

$$\Delta Y_t == \alpha + p^* Y_{t-1} + \varepsilon_t \quad (5)$$

The Phillips-Perron unit root test is also based on the t-statistics that are associated with the estimated coefficients of p^*

ARDL Bound Testing Approach

To investigate the long-run and short-run dynamics between the variables, the ARDL bounds developed by Pesaran and Pesaran (1997), Pesaran and Shin (1999), and Pesaran *et al.* (2000, 2001) were chosen. The ARDL approach has many advantages over other cointegration methods. ARDL may apply irrespective of whether the underlying variables are purely 1(0), 1(1), or mutually cointegrated (Pesaran and Shin, 1999). The ARDL approach has estimated better small-sample properties (Huang,2002). In the ARDL procedure, the estimation of the results is even possible if the explanatory variables are endogenous. The empirical ARDL equation is formulated as follows:

$$\Delta CO2_{it} = \beta_0 + \beta_{1k}\sum_{k=1}^{n}\Delta CO2_{t-k} + \beta_{2k}\sum_{k=1}^{n}\Delta FDI_{(t-k)} + \beta_{3k}\sum_{k=1}^{n}\Delta \mathrm{GDP}_{(t-k)} + \beta_{4k}\sum_{k=1}^{n}\Delta HCI_{I(t-k)} + \beta_{5k}\sum_{k=1}^{n}\Delta URB_{(t-k)} + \lambda_1 CO2_{(t-1)} + \lambda_2 FDI_{(t-1)} + \lambda_3 GDP_{(t-1)} + \lambda_4 HCI_{(t-1)} + \lambda_5 URB_{(t-1)} + \varepsilon_{1t} \quad (6)$$

Where Δ indicates the first difference, β_0 is a constant, ε is the residual, β_1, β_2, β_3, β_4 & β_5 are the short-run coefficients, while λ_1, λ_2, λ_3, λ_4 & λ_5 are the long-run coefficients. We estimate the long-run relationship between the variables by testing the null hypothesis of no co-integration $H_0 = \lambda_1 = \lambda_2 = \lambda_3 = \lambda_4 = \lambda_5 = 0$ against the alternative hypothesis $H_1 = \lambda_1 \neq \lambda_2 \neq \lambda_3 \neq \lambda_4 \neq \lambda_5 \neq 0$. The F-statistic value is used to determine the cointegration. The critical values given by Pesaran *et al.* (2001) show whether to accept or reject the null hypothesis. If the F-statistic values lie within the critical values, the result will be inconclusive, while in the case the F-statistic lies above the critical values, the result will be considered conclusive; however, an F-statistic lower than the critical value means no co-integration.

If the long-run relationship between CO_2, Y, HCI, and URB exists, then we estimate the long-run coefficients. The following empirical equation will be used to estimate the long-run coefficients.

$$\Delta CO2_{it} = \varphi_0 + \varphi_1\sum_{i=1}^{0} CO2_{t-1} + \varphi_2\sum_{i=1}^{0} FDI_{t-1} + \varphi_3\sum_{i=1}^{0} GDP_{t-1} + \varphi_4\sum_{i=1}^{0} HCI_{t-1} + \varphi_5\sum_{i=1}^{0} URB_{t-1} + \mu_t \quad (7)$$

If this study finds evidence of a long-run relationship between ecological footprints, economic growth, growth square, human capital, and renewable energy, then to estimate the short-run coefficients, the following empirical equation will be employed.

$$\Delta CO2_{t} = \delta_0 + \delta_1\sum_{i=1}^{0} \Delta CO2_{t-1} + \delta_2\sum_{i=1}^{0} FDI_{t-1} + \delta_3\sum_{i=1}^{0} \Delta GDP_{t-1} + \delta_4\sum_{i=1}^{0} \Delta HCI_{t-1} + \delta_5\sum_{i=1}^{0} \Delta URB_{t-1} + +\eta EC_{t-1} + \mu_t \quad (8)$$

The error correction model shows the speed of adjustment needed to restore the long-run equilibrium following a short-run shock. The n is the coefficient of the error correction term in the equation that indicates the speed of adjustments.

RESULTS AND DISCUSSIONS

Using a data-driven approach, this study searched for patterns linking financial development, economic growth, urbanization, and human capital with environmental outcomes. A special modelling technique helped us capture both the immediate and long-term environmental impacts. The descriptive statistics presented in Table **2** reveal notable trends across key variables from 1990 to 2019, reflecting the economic and environmental shifts in China, Japan, India, South Korea, and Indonesia. Carbon emissions (LNCO2) have shown a marked increase, rising from a mean of -0.437944 in 1990-91 to 2.503503 in 2018-19. This increase underscores the moderate yet steady rise in pollution levels due to industrialization in these economies. The small deviation from the mean, with a standard deviation of 0.967255, indicates high stability in CO_2 levels overall, although significant disparities exist, as industrialized economies like China contribute higher emissions compared to less-industrialized ones like Indonesia. Financial inclusion, as measured by the Financial Development Index (LNFDI), has experienced a moderate decrease, shifting from -1.456335 in 1990-91 to -0.096025 in 2018-19. The median value of LNFDI (-0.554013) being slightly higher than the mean (-0.659505) suggests that most economies in the sample have better-than-average financial inclusion, though still limited. GDP per capita (LNGDP) shows a high mean value of 8.593081, reflective of the robust economic output across these nations.

Table 2. Descriptive statistics.

Statistics	Variables				
	LNCO2	**LNFDI**	**LNGDP**	**LNHC**	**LNUP**
Mean	1.267915	-0.659505	8.593081	0.934327	3.939147
Median	1.435814	-0.554013	8.235074	0.876841	3.941969
Maximum	2.503503	-0.096025	10.49511	1.325781	4.518501
Minimum	-0.437944	-1.456335	6.270796	0.396708	3.240520
Std. Dev.	0.967255	0.427988	1.399342	0.253336	0.435607
Skewness	-0.208859	-0.331743	0.040171	-0.101958	-0.124065
Kurtosis	1.445028	1.580249	1.503351	1.837091	1.477165
Jarque-Bera	16.20265	15.34942	14.04009	8.712114	14.87872
Probability	0.000303	0.000464	0.000894	0.012829	0.000588

(Table 2) cont.....

Statistics	Variables				
	LNCO2	LNFDI	LNGDP	LNHC	LNUP
Sum	190.1873	-98.92579	1288.962	140.1490	590.8720
Sum Sq. Dev.	139.4018	27.29294	291.7657	9.562690	28.27324
Observations	150	150	150	150	150

Source: Authors calculation.

Human Capital (LNHC) indicates sustained growth, moving from 0.396708 in 1990-91 to 1.325781 in 2018-19, pointing to consistent improvements in education and skill development. Meanwhile, urbanization (LNUP) has a high mean level of 3.939147, characteristic of dense urban populations, with a moderate standard deviation of 0.435607, which highlights varying stages of urban development within the sample economies. Collectively, these statistics underscore the heterogeneity among these Asian economies regarding industrialization, financial inclusion, and urbanization, reinforcing the need for differentiated strategies for sustainable development.

The ARDL model applied in this study assesses the relationship between per capita CO_2 emissions (LNCO2) and multiple influencing factors, namely financial development (LNFDI), GDP per capita (LNGDP), human capital (LNHC), and urban population (LNUP). To check the stationarity of variables, the Augmented Dickey Fuller technique was utilized; all the variables of the model satisfied the stationarity check by being stationary either at the level or first difference. This paved the way to run the ARDL model in the study. The results offer insights into how financial development and economic growth impact environmental sustainability in these emerging Asian economies.

The long-run relationship analysis in Table **3** and **4** reveals that financial development, with a coefficient of 0.322820, has a weakly significant positive effect on CO_2 emissions, suggesting that financial expansion may contribute to environmental degradation in the leading emerging Asian economies. This result aligns with studies by Zhang and Cheng (2009), Saud *et al.* (2020), Sethi *et al.* (2020), and Zu (2022). Thus, while financial inclusion is essential for economic growth, stringent environmental regulations are needed to ensure that this growth does not come at the cost of environmental quality.

Human capital also shows a positive relationship with CO_2 emissions, where a 1% increase in human capital correlates with an 8.78% rise in emissions. This result indicates that human capital in these economies has not yet fostered sustainability, echoing the findings of De Qiang *et al.* (2022). In these cases, the skills and education currently prioritized may not effectively support sustainable practices, highlighting an area for policy intervention to redirect human capital towards environmentally sustainable outcomes.

GDP growth, on the other hand, demonstrates a negative coefficient of -1.078955, indicating that higher GDP per capita is associated with lower CO_2 emissions. This suggests that as these economies grow, they tend to adopt more sustainable practices, contributing positively to environmental quality in the long term. This result provides a favorable outlook for the potential of economic growth to be compatible with environmental sustainability, which contrasts with concerns about the environmental impacts of rapid growth.

In contrast, urban population growth has a positive and significant impact on CO_2 emissions, with a 1% increase in urban population leading to a 3.24% rise in emissions. This trend suggests that urbanization in these economies contributes substantially to emissions increases, emphasizing the environmental challenges posed by dense urban centers. As urban areas expand, policies focusing on green urban planning and emission reduction are crucial to counteract the environmental pressures linked to urbanization in these rapidly developing regions.

In the short-run analysis based on equation (8), financial development (LNFD) demonstrates a negative impact on carbon emissions, with a coefficient of -0.094734, indicating that increased financial development can help reduce emissions in the short term. Similarly, human capital (LNHC) has a small yet negative coefficient of -26.09158, suggesting that human capital also contributes to environmental sustainability in the short run.

However, both GDP growth (LNGDP) and urban population (LNUP) positively impact carbon emissions in the short term. This indicates that economic expansion and urbanization initially add to environmental pressures, reflecting the immediate resource demands and increased emissions associated with rapid growth and urban development. These findings suggest that while financial development and human capital have potential roles in promoting short-term environmental sustainability, efforts are required to extend these benefits into the long run. This transition is crucial to support sustainable growth that balances economic advancement with environmental quality.

SUMMARY AND POLICY RECOMMENDATION

In the long run, financial development and urban population positively affect CO_2 emissions, while GDP per capita appears to reduce emissions, potentially reflecting environmental improvements as economies grow. Human capital, on the other hand, is positively associated with emissions in the long run. Short-run effects of the independent variables on CO_2 emissions are mostly insignificant, and the model does not show a significant speed of adjustment to equilibrium (indicated by the error correction term). This suggests that changes in these factors may influence emissions more over the long term than in the short term. In fast-growing economies like China and India, where financial development often drives small business growth and industrial expansion, more people having access to funds has led to greater energy use and pollution. Meanwhile, in Japan and South Korea, where financial systems often support green projects (like loans for solar panels or energy-efficient equipment), financial development has actually helped reduce emissions. So, financial development can lead to either positive or negative outcomes for the environment, depending on whether the financing promotes sustainability. Economic growth and the environment have a complicated relationship in these countries. In places like China and Indonesia, rising income levels have led to more industrial activity, pushing up pollution. But in Japan and South Korea, which are more economically developed, emissions are starting to drop as these countries invest in cleaner, more efficient technologies. This pattern backs up the idea that economic growth initially harms the environment but can eventually lead to sustainability as income rises. Investing in education and workforce skills makes a big difference for environmental health, especially in Japan and South Korea. With well-educated workforces, these countries are now leading in industries focused on clean technologies, which reduces their carbon footprints. But in countries like India and Indonesia, it's still a challenge to translate educational gains into environmental improvements, largely because access to education and green job opportunities varies widely.

To make financial development work for the environment, governments could create policies that encourage green investments. For example, banks could offer lower interest rates for projects that focus on renewable energy or waste reduction. Countries experiencing rapid growth, like China and India, could offer incentives for industries to adopt greener practices. This could include subsidies for energy-efficient equipment or tax breaks for companies that reduce emissions. Investing in education programs focused on environmental science and technology can make a big difference. By giving workers the skills they need for green jobs, countries can build a future that is both prosperous and environmentally responsible. To sum it up, financial development, economic growth, and human capital have a major impact on environmental health in Asia's top economies. When designed carefully, policies that promote inclusive growth, sustainable finance, and education in green skills can help these countries strike a balance between economic success and environmental responsibility. This chapter highlights the importance of customized, thoughtful policies that make it possible for these economies to thrive without sacrificing the planet.

APPENDIX:

Table 3. ARDL long-run results.

Variable	Coefficient	Std. Error	t-statistic	Prob.
LNFD	0.322820	0.185293	1.742215	0.0890
LNGDP	-1.078955	0.413984	-2.606272	0.0127
LNHC	8.770915	2.060368	4.256966	0.0001
LNUP	3.248029	1.137481	2.855457	0.0067

Source: Authors Calculation.

Table 4. ARDL short-run results.

Variable	Coefficient	Std. Error	t-statistic	Prob.
LNCO2	-0.623935	0.463530	-1.346051	0.1857
LNFD	-0.094734	0.208487	-0.454389	0.6519
LNGDP	0.162979	0.414677	0.393026	0.6963
LNHC	-26.09158	20.40640	-1.278598	0.2082
LNUP	0.367072	15.27006	0.024039	0.9809

Source: Authors Calculation.

REFERENCES

Ali, K., Jianguo, Du, Kirikkaleli, D., (2023). How do energy resources and financial development cause environmental sustainability? *Energy Reports, 9,* 4036-4048. ISSN 2352-4847.
[http://dx.doi.org/10.1016/j.egyr.2023.03.040]

Baochang, Xu., Sihui, Li., Ayesha, Afzal, Nawazish, Mirza., Meng, Zhang (2022). The impact of financial development on environmental sustainability: A European perspective. *Resources Policy, 78*(102814), 0301-4207.
[http://dx.doi.org/10.1016/j.resourpol.2022.102814]

Du, Q., Wu, N., Zhang, F., Lei, Y., Saeed, A. (2022). Impact of financial inclusion and human capital on environmental quality: evidence from emerging economies. *Environmental Science and Pollution Research, 29*(22), 33033-33045.
[http://dx.doi.org/10.1007/s11356-021-17945-x] [PMID: 35025039]

Kirikkaleli, D., & Adebayo, T. S. (2021). Do renewable energy consumption and financial development matter for environmental sustainability? New global evidence. *Sustainable Development., 29*(4), 583–594.
[http://dx.doi.org/10.1002/sd.2159]

Lee, C.C., Zhou, B., Yang, T.Y., Yu, C.H., Zhao, J. (2023). The impact of urbanization on CO2 emissions in China: the key role of foreign direct investment. *Emerging Markets Finance and Trade, 59*(2), 451-462.
[http://dx.doi.org/10.1080/1540496X.2022.2106843]

Le, T.H., Chuc, A.T., Taghizadeh-Hesary, F. (2019). Financial inclusion and its impact on financial efficiency and sustainability: Empirical evidence from Asia. *Borsa Istanbul Review, 19*(4), 310-322.
[http://dx.doi.org/10.1016/j.bir.2019.07.002]

Le, T.H., Le, H.C., Taghizadeh-Hesary, F. (2020). Does financial inclusion impact CO_2 emissions? Evidence from Asia. *Finance Research Letters., 34,* 101451..

[http://dx.doi.org/10.1016/j.frl.2020.101451]

Saud, S., Chen, S., Haseeb, A., Sumayya, (2020). The role of financial development and globalization in the environment: Accounting ecological footprint indicators for selected one-belt-one-road initiative countries. *Journal of Cleaner Production, 250*, 119518.
[http://dx.doi.org/10.1016/j.jclepro.2019.119518]

Sethi, P., Chakrabarti, D., & Bhattacharjee, S. (2020). Globalization, financial development and economic growth: Perils on the environmental sustainability of an emerging economy *Journal of Policy Modeling, 42*(3), 520-535. ISSN 0161-8938.
[http://dx.doi.org/10.1016/j.jpolmod.2020.01.007]

Uche, E., Effiom, L. (2021). Financial development and environmental sustainability in Nigeria: fresh insights from multiple threshold nonlinear ARDL model. *Environmental Science and Pollution Research International, 28*(29), 39524-39539.
[http://dx.doi.org/10.1007/s11356-021-12843-8] [PMID: 33754273]

World Population Review. (2024). *GDP Ranked by Country.* Available from: https://worldpopulationreview.com/countries/by-gdp

Woodruff, J. (2019). Factors affecting economic development and growth. Small Business - Chron. Available from: https://smallbusiness.chron.com/factors-affecting-economic-development-growth-1517.html

Wu, L., Adebayo, T.S., Yue, X.G., Umut, A. (2023). The role of renewable energy consumption and financial development in environmental sustainability: implications for the Nordic Countries. *International Journal of Sustainable Development & World Ecology, 30*(1), 21-36.
[http://dx.doi.org/10.1080/13504509.2022.2115577]

Zhang, X.P., Cheng, X.M. (2009). Energy consumption, carbon emissions, and economic growth in China. *Ecological Economics, 68*(10), 2706-2712.
[http://dx.doi.org/10.1016/j.ecolecon.2009.05.011]

Zafar, M.W., Saud, S., Hou, F. (2019). The impact of globalization and financial development on environmental quality: evidence from selected countries in the Organization for Economic Co-operation and Development (OECD). *Environmental Science and Pollution Research, 26*(13), 13246-13262. a
[http://dx.doi.org/10.1007/s11356-019-04761-7] [PMID: 30900127]

Zins, A., Weill, L. (2016). The determinants of financial inclusion in Africa. *Review of Development Finance, 6*(1), 46-57.
[http://dx.doi.org/10.1016/j.rdf.2016.05.001]

CHAPTER 7

Financial Technology (FinTech) as a Game Changer for Financial Inclusion

Mohammed Majeed[1,*], **Abibu Amidu**[2], **Sofia Devi Shamurailatpam**[3] and **Vijaya Kittu Manda**[4]

[1] *Department of Marketing, Tamale Technical University, Tamale, Ghana*

[2] *Department of Accountancy, Tamale Technical University, Tamale, Ghana*

[3] *Department of Banking and Insurance, Faculty of Commerce, The Maharaja Sayajirao University of Baroda, Vadodara, Gujarat, India*

[4] *Perspectives on Business Management & Economics, Visakhapatnam, Andhra Pradesh, India*

Abstract: Financial technology (FinTech) has materialized as a transformative force in improving financial inclusion, particularly in emerging markets. By leveraging improvements such as mobile banking, MoMo, digital payment platforms, and data analytics, Fintech has expanded access to financial services for underserved populations. This paper examines the role of Fintech in promoting financial inclusion, highlighting its impact on economic development and poverty reduction. It also addresses the challenges and risks associated with Fintech implementation, including cybersecurity concerns, regulatory hurdles, and the potential for amplified disparity. The study underscores the need for a balanced style that fosters innovation while guaranteeing buyer protection and financial stability.

Keywords: Financial inclusion, Fintech, Financial, Innovation, Technology.

INTRODUCTION

In recent years, financial technology (Fintech) has emerged as a key player in the realm of financial inclusion. Over the past two decades, financial inclusion has become a primary objective for developing nations' financial sectors (Lensink *et al.*, 2022). This shift from focusing on financial development, which measures the overall size of the financial sector, to financial inclusion, which emphasizes broader access to and use of financial services, represents a significant move towards more socially nuanced indicators. Many experts believe that affordable, widespread digital solutions are crucial for reaching the 1.7 billion individuals

* **Corresponding author Mohammed Majeed:** Department of Marketing, Tamale Technical University, Tamale, Ghana; E-mail:tunteya14june@gmail.com

worldwide who remain excluded from formal financial services (Triodos Investment Management, 2019). The growth of fintech initiatives and related investments has been substantial.

Currently, financial inclusion is recognized as a crucial factor in achieving seven of the seventeen Sustainable Development Goals (World Bank, 2018) and has long been considered essential for optimal societal participation in economic and social spheres (Anderloni *et al.*, 2008). Notably, research has established clear causal connections between women's financial inclusion and their economic empowerment (Duvendack & Mader, 2020). Fintech refers to new technologies that enhance and streamline the delivery and utilization of financial services. At its core, fintech employs specialized software and algorithms on computers and smartphones to help businesses, entrepreneurs, and consumers better manage their financial operations and lives.

Fintech is revolutionizing how individuals handle their finances, enabling them to conduct transactions anytime and anywhere through various platforms (Yang and Zhang 2022). By leveraging technology, fintech companies are creating innovative and user-friendly channels for financial services. This technological advancement is particularly impactful in areas with limited traditional banking infrastructure, allowing people to perform financial transactions using their smartphones (Asif *et al.* 2023). Fintech services are generally more cost-effective than traditional financial services (Shaikh *et al.* 2023), making them more accessible and affordable to a broader population and significantly impacting financial inclusion. In developing nations like India, promoting digital financial literacy is crucial to ensure widespread access to financial services.

There is a growing possibility that fintech-driven entities may emerge as viable alternatives to traditional financial intermediaries, markets, and infrastructures. While the widespread adoption of modern technologies offers numerous benefits, it also presents certain risks. Fintech has the potential to increase efficiency in the financial sector, provide more targeted and improved products and services, and expand financial inclusion in developing regions. However, it may also pose risks if its implementation undermines competition, trust, monetary policy transmission, and financial stability. Financial inclusion is essential for the well-being of households, the growth of businesses, and the advancement of national economies. Recent research has mainly focused on three areas: developing measures for financial inclusion, investigating the determinants that affect it, and assessing its impacts. However, the role of financial technology (fintech) in enhancing financial inclusion is a relatively new yet significant area that warrants further exploration. This chapter aims to provide an introductory overview of how fintech is transforming financial inclusion in the financial industry and enhancing the efficiency of the broader economy. This chapter holds particular importance for developing and emerging markets by examining the challenges and issues surrounding fintech's role in enhancing financial inclusion within complex institutional environments. Additionally, it seeks to expand the current knowledge base regarding FinTech usage and financial inclusion while providing actionable recommendations for industry stakeholders and policymakers alike.

LITERATURE REVIEW

FinTech

FinTech, a fusion of the words "financial" and "technology," emerged during the 2007-2008 financial crisis and has since transformed the financial services industry with new technological advancements. Modern banking growth is largely built on two core elements: technology-driven banking systems and innovations. In India, the expansion of mobile networks in previously underserved regions over the past decade has been instrumental in this evolution (Abubakari *et al.*, 2025). Payment banks have also emerged as an alternative to online and mobile banking, enhancing operational efficiency and lowering customer service costs in rural and semi-urban areas.

FinTech refers to the innovations designed to compete with traditional financial methods and improve the delivery of financial services. FinTech companies aim to reach a broader audience more efficiently, affordably, and in a customer-centric manner compared to traditional financial institutions (Triodos Investment Management, 2019). These innovations have greatly enhanced financial service accessibility. Services like M-Pesa have given millions access to previously unavailable financial services (Demirgüç-Kunt *et al.*, 2018; Central Bank of Kenya, 2020). Additionally, FinTech has reduced transaction costs, making services more affordable for low-income users by eliminating the need for physical infrastructure (Gabor & Brooks, 2016; Ozili, 2018). Today, FinTech services encompass savings, loans, and insurance products, leading to increased financial inclusion rates in Kenya (FSD Kenya, 2019; Cook & McKay, 2015).

Financial Inclusion

Financial inclusion, which refers to ensuring that financial services are accessible and affordable for everyone, is vital for economic development. The World Bank (2022) estimates that about 1.4 billion adults worldwide are unbanked, with most of them residing in low-income nations and rural areas. Traditional banking systems often struggle to serve these populations due to high operational costs and logistical difficulties. Financial inclusion ensures that individuals and businesses have access to essential financial services—such as payments, savings, credit, and insurance—that are tailored to their needs and delivered in a responsible, sustainable manner. According to a 2017 World Bank report, the number of people without banking services dropped from 2 billion in 2014 to approximately 1.7 billion in 2017. Despite these advancements, significant challenges remain, especially regarding the availability of financial institutions. Overcoming these obstacles is essential for improving the quality of life for marginalized populations in developing countries. Financial technology plays a critical role in expanding financial services to previously underserved segments of society.

FinTech and Financial Inclusion

FinTech enables customers in underserved or rural areas to access financial services through digital platforms, eliminating the need for physical bank branches (Arner *et al.*, 2020). By offering convenience and affordability, FinTech reduces the costs typically associated with traditional banking services (Shen *et al.*, 2020). This makes financial services more accessible to a wider audience, including those who are not technologically inclined or previously excluded from formal financial systems (Bongomin & Munene, 2021; Senyo & Osabutey, 2020). Through services like microfinance and peer-to-peer lending, FinTech helps small businesses and individuals who may not qualify for conventional loans access financial support, thus promoting economic activity and entrepreneurship in underserved communities (Björkegren & Grissen, 2018). Additionally, FinTech companies often partner with governments to implement financial inclusion initiatives, streamlining the disbursement of social benefits, subsidies, and other financial assistance (Asif *et al.*, 2023). By leveraging technology, FinTech is breaking down barriers to formal financial systems, making these services more inclusive and accessible (Aleemi *et al.*, 2023).

Personalization for Customer Experience

Fintech companies are increasingly adopting hyper-personalization strategies to tailor financial products and services to individual customer needs and preferences. By leveraging advanced data analytics and artificial intelligence, these firms gain deep insights into customer behavior, enabling them to offer personalized recommendations and customized solutions. For instance, a company might provide a shorter repayment term to a woman who owns a seasonal business or offer a lower interest rate to a woman with a strong loan repayment history. Digital lending platforms utilize alternative data sources to assess creditworthiness, while robo-advisors deliver investment strategies aligned with investors' risk profiles and financial goals. This level of hyper-personalization not only enhances customer satisfaction but also promotes greater financial literacy, empowering consumers to make informed decisions.

Addressing Challenges

While financial technology offers significant opportunities, it also presents substantial risks, particularly for consumers with limited income. These risks encompass inadequate cybersecurity and data protection, excessive pricing, irresponsible lending practices, and potential scams.

Enhancing Accessibility and Cost-effectiveness

Technology-driven financial solutions, including mobile devices, data analysis, innovative digital offerings and strategies, and the implementation of agent networks, have the capacity to dramatically improve and promote financial inclusion. These advancements operate at a considerably faster pace and broader scale compared to conventional financial inclusion entities. Such technology-enabled approaches play a crucial role in lowering operational expenses, boosting efficiency, and reaching individuals in distant and rural locations. Financial technology companies have broadened their focus beyond traditional microcredit offerings. They are leveraging technology to create, tailor, and distribute a wider array of financial products suited to low-income individuals' needs, such as micro-insurance, micro-savings, and money transfer services. These innovations can assist financially excluded individuals in establishing credit histories, enabling them to access the financial system. Additionally, they can support those struggling with financial obligations by combining debts, offering more favorable interest rates, and providing personalized guidance to help over-indebted clients achieve financial stability. Financial technology holds the potential to exponentially increase financial inclusion.

Customized Offerings through Service Disaggregation

Financial technology companies are breaking down traditional banking services into individual components. While conventional banks typically bundle savings accounts, checking accounts, and credit cards together, fintech firms often provide these services separately. This approach allows customers to select only the services they desire, which is particularly advantageous for women seeking personalized financial solutions and increased flexibility. For example, companies like Dvara SmartGold offer small-scale savings and investment products to women in rural areas, enabling them to save money and invest in gold.

Eliminating Geographic Barriers

The rise of mobile banking and online platforms has extended financial services to remote areas previously lacking access. For example, companies such as MoMo in Ghana and M-Pesa in Kenya have transformed how rural populations handle and transfer funds. This development is not merely a matter of convenience; it's about fostering economic growth in previously underserved regions.

Expanding Financial Inclusion through Affordable Solutions and Services

Fintech leverages cutting-edge technologies to provide alternatives that frequently reduce traditional banking costs, enabling individuals with limited resources to participate. For instance, online-exclusive banks, known as "neobanks," have minimized overhead expenses, transferring these savings to customers through reduced fees.

Smartphone Banking

Smartphone banking transforms common devices into virtual financial centers, allowing individuals to manage their finances from any location at any time. This has been especially revolutionary in areas lacking conventional banking infrastructure. Through smartphone banking, users can conduct transactions, set aside money, and even make investments—all using their mobile devices. However, it's crucial to note that not everyone has access to the internet or owns a smartphone, highlighting the ongoing need for expanded outreach and infrastructure development.

Peer-to-Peer Lending Platforms

Peer-to-peer lending platforms are reshaping the financial landscape by directly linking borrowers with lenders. The result? Increased access to credit and often more advantageous terms for both parties. Take Tala, for example, which empowers underbanked populations in nations such as Mexico, the Philippines, Kenya, and India by offering a range of digital financial services to assist them in borrowing, saving, and growing their assets.

Small-Scale Insurance

Small-scale insurance emerges as a ray of hope for populations underserved by mainstream insurance providers. These offerings provide simplified, low-cost coverage tailored to specific needs, offering a safety net to the most vulnerable individuals. Whether it's protection against crop failure or unexpected illness, small-scale insurance helps individuals and communities build resilience against unforeseen challenges.

Improving Financial Education

Technology platforms are being utilized by fintech companies to boost financial literacy in India, particularly among disadvantaged groups and women. These firms provide educational content, including articles, videos, and infographics, to teach individuals about financial principles such as budgeting, saving, and investing. They also offer individualized financial advice to their customers and employ 'gamification' techniques to make learning about finance more interactive and appealing. The National Bank for Agriculture and Rural Development has created Saksham, a mobile application available in multiple languages, which educates rural clients, including women's self-help groups, on various financial topics like saving, investing, borrowing, and insurance.

Expanding Financial Accessibility

Financial services organizations leverage technology to provide microloans to small-scale entrepreneurs and rural women who often lack traditional collateral. These firms assess creditworthiness using non-traditional data, such as mobile phone usage and transaction history. Companies like Kisan Network and Jai Kisan focus on farmers, offering mobile platforms for obtaining agricultural inputs, credit, and crucial market information. Digital wallets provided by companies such as Phonepe and Paytm enable cashless transactions, empowering individuals without traditional bank accounts to manage payments, receive remittances, and access essential services conveniently and securely.

Promoting Efficiency and Inclusivity

FinTechs can help introduce more efficient and inclusive business models and broaden the range of financial service providers. The significant potential of FinTech to create a more inclusive financial system and drive economic growth is widely acknowledged. A study by the McKinsey Global Institute (Manyika *et al.* 2016) estimates that emerging economies could increase their GDP by $3.7 trillion by 2025 through full adoption of digital finance. Research has also demonstrated that countries with higher levels of financial inclusion experience stronger GDP growth rates and lower income inequality (Ravi, 2019).

Lowering Financial Service Costs

Fintech firms have decreased the cost of financial services by utilizing technology and eliminating physical infrastructure and operational expenses. Platforms like Paytm and Google Pay offer low-cost or free transactions, bypassing traditional processors. Robo-advisors provide affordable portfolio management, making professional investment advice more accessible. Peer-to-peer lending reduces interest rates, benefiting both borrowers and lenders. Innovative companies like Paynearby partner with micro-entrepreneurs to extend financial services to rural customers, including women.

Implications

The integration of fintech into the financial services sector has several significant implications:

1. **Economic Empowerment**: Fintech solutions provide marginalized communities with access to essential financial services, enabling them to participate more fully in the economy. This access facilitates entrepreneurship, savings, and investment, contributing to poverty alleviation and economic growth.
2. **Cost Reduction**: By utilizing technology, fintech reduces the costs associated with traditional banking, making financial services more affordable and accessible. This reduction is particularly beneficial for low-income individuals who have been excluded from conventional financial systems.
3. **Regulatory Challenges**: The swift advancement of fintech presents challenges for regulators in ensuring consumer safety, data privacy, and systemic stability. Developing suitable regulatory frameworks that balance innovation with risk management is crucial.
4. **Risk of Exclusion**: While fintech has the possibility to enhance inclusion, there is a risk that certain groups, such as the elderly or those without internet access, may be further marginalized. Addressing digital literacy and infrastructure gaps is essential to ensure equitable access.

CONCLUSION

Fintech stands as a pivotal driver in advancing financial inclusion, offering innovative solutions that bridge gaps left by traditional banking systems. Its role in providing accessible, affordable, and tailored financial services has the potential to transform economies and improve livelihoods. However, realizing this potential requires careful navigation of associated risks and challenges. Policymakers, industry stakeholders, and regulators must collaborate to create an environment that supports fintech innovation while safeguarding consumer interests and maintaining financial system integrity. Through such collaborative efforts, fintech can be harnessed to achieve broader financial inclusion and contribute to sustainable economic development.

REFERENCES

Abubakari, A.-R., Majeed, M., Alhassan, N., & Yomboi, J. (Eds.). (2025.). *Navigating the Fintech frontier: Transformative innovations and risk factors in financial services.* Bentham Science Publishers.. [http://dx.doi.org/10.2174/97898153249071250101]

Aleemi, A.R., Javaid, F., Hafeez, S.S. (2023). *Finclusion*: The nexus of Fintech and financial inclusion against banks' market power. *Heliyon, 9*(12), e22551. [http://dx.doi.org/10.1016/j.heliyon.2023.e22551] [PMID: 38213587]

Arner, D.W., Buckley, R.P., Zetzsche, D.A., Veidt, R. (2020). Sustainability, FinTech and financial inclusion. *European Business Organization Law Review, 21*(1), 7-35. [http://dx.doi.org/10.1007/s40804-020-00183-y]

Asif, M., Khan, M.N., Tiwari, S., Wani, S.K., Alam, F. (2023). The impact of Fintech and digital financial services on financial inclusion in India. *Journal of Risk and Financial Management, 16*(2), 122. [http://dx.doi.org/10.3390/jrfm16020122]

Björkegren, D., Grissen, D. (2018). The potential of digital credit to bank the poor. *AEA Papers and Proceedings, 108*, 68-71. [http://dx.doi.org/10.1257/pandp.20181032]

Bongomin, G.O.C., Ntayi, J.M. (2020). Mobile money adoption and usage and financial inclusion: Mediating effect of digital consumer protection. *Digital Policy, Regulation and Governance, 22*(3), 157-176.

Central Bank of Kenya. (2018). *Annual report and financial statements for the year ended 30 June 2018.* Available from: http://libraryir.parliament.go.ke/handle/123456789/34329.

Central Bank of Kenya. (2020). *Annual report and financial statements for the year ended 30 June 2020.* available from: https://www.centralbank.go.ke/uploads/cbk_annual_reports/1456103982_ANNUAL%20REPORT%202020%20Posted%20on%20Website.pdf.

Cook, T., & McKay, C. (2015). *How M-Shwari works: The story so far.* CGAP and FSD Kenya. [https://www.cgap.org/sites/default/files/Forum-How-M-Shwari-Works-Apr-2015.pdf].

Demirgüç-Kunt, A., Klapper, L., Singer, D., Ansar, S., Hess, J. (2018). *The Global Findex Database 2017: Measuring financial inclusion and the Fintech revolution.* World Bank. [http://dx.doi.org/10.1596/978-1-4648-1259-0]

Central Bank of Kenya (CBK), Kenya National Bureau of Statistics (KNBS), & Financial Sector Deepening (FSD) Kenya. (2024). *FinAccess Household Survey Report.* Available from: https://www.centralbank.go.ke/wp-content/uploads/2024/12/202--FINACCESS-HOUSEHOLD-SURVEY-MAIN-REPORT.pdf.

Gabor, D., Brooks, S. (2017). The digital revolution in financial inclusion: international development in the fintech era. *New Political Economy, 22*(4), 423-436. [http://dx.doi.org/10.1080/13563467.2017.1259298]

Gupta, K., Chaudhary, A. (2023). How Fintech can enable financial inclusion and reduce gender gaps in India. *Asian Development Blog.* Available from: https://blogs.adb.org/blog/how-

Okello Candiya Bongomin, G., Munene, J.C. (2021). Analyzing the relationship between mobile money adoption and usage and financial inclusion of MSMEs in developing countries: Mediating role of cultural norms in Uganda. *Journal of African Business, 22*(1), 1-20. [http://dx.doi.org/10.1080/15228916.2019.1695189]

Ozili, P.K. (2018). Impact of digital finance on financial inclusion and stability. *Borsa Istanbul Review, 18*(4), 329-340. [http://dx.doi.org/10.1016/j.bir.2017.12.003]

Ravi, S. (2019). Accelerating financial inclusion in India. Brookings India Report. Available from: https://www.brookings.edu/articles/accelerating-financial-inclusion-in-india/.

Senyo, P.K., Osabutey, E.L.C. (2020). Unearthing antecedents to financial inclusion through FinTech innovations. *Technovation, 98*, 102155. [http://dx.doi.org/10.1016/j.technovation.2020.102155]

Shen, Y., Hu, W., Hueng, C.J. (2018). The effects of financial literacy, digital financial product usage and internet usage on financial inclusion in China. In *MATEC Web of Conferences, 228,* 05012. EDP Sciences.

Triodos Investment Management (2019). *Fintech: A game changer for financial inclusion.* Available from: www.triodos-im.com/inclusivefinance

Klapper, L., Singer, D., Starita, L., & Norris, A. (2025). *The Global Findex Database 2025: Connectivity and financial inclusion in the digital economy.* World Bank. https://www.worldbank.org/en/publication/globalfindex.

SUBJECT INDEX

Mohammed Majeed, Sofia Devi Shamurailatpam, Parag Sunil Shukla, Ibrahim Osman & Hamidu Gafaru Dokurugu (Eds.)

J

K

L

M

N

P

R

S

T

U

V

W

www.ingramcontent.com/pod-product-compliance
Lightning Source LLC
LaVergne TN
LVHW070953210926
848482LV00002B/202